LEARNING TO BE 85

LEARNING TO BE 85

Elizabeth Welch

UPPER
ROOM BOOKS
NASHVILLE

LEARNING TO BE 85

Scripture quotations designated KJV are from the King James Version of the
Bible.

Scripture quotations designated RSV are from the Revised Standard Version of
the Bible, copyright 1946, 1952, and © 1971 by the Division of Christian
Education, National Council of the Churches of Christ in the United States of
America, and are used by permission.

Scripture quotations designated NEB are from the *New English Bible,* © The
Delegates of the Oxford University Press and the Syndics of the Cambridge
University Press 1961 and 1970, and are reprinted by permission.

"Jis' Blue" by Etta Baldwin Oldham from *Poetry Arranged for the Speaking
Choir.* Used by permission of Expression Company.

Photo on page 127 courtesy of *The Winston-Salem Journal.*

Cover design: Jim Bateman
First Printing: October 1991 (5)
ISBN 0-8358-0649-9
Library of Congress Catalog Card Number: 91-65728

Printed in the United States of America

To my mother and father, who gave me everything that mattered.

"Silver and gold have I none; but such as I have give I thee."
(Acts 3:6, KJV)

Contents

I will not be negligent to put you always in remembrance of these
things, though you know them . . . Yea, I think it meet
. . . to stir you up by putting you in remembrance.
(2 Peter 1:12-13, KJV)

Foreword

Every now and then you take up a book just to read for a few minutes, and you become so fascinated and so involved in it that you just can't put it down. Finally, when you have finished reading, you become completely conscious of the fact that you will never forget the story. It is an amazing feeling. That experience has been mine three times.

The first book to touch me so deeply was *The Nazarene,* by Sholem Asch. Reading it was a converting experience that affects me still. The second book to become a part of my mind and soul was *The Keys of the Kingdom,* by A.J. Cronin, and the third work is this one, *Learning to Be 85,* by Elizabeth Welch. I wondered at first if it was my close friendship with the author that influenced me to this degree. You see, I was her pastor for three years prior to my election to the episcopacy. I witnessed her intense loyalty to her church and to its minister. I also knew she was a brilliant member of a fine college faculty, one of the oldest and most sophisticated colleges in America. I could have been swayed by any of these reasons, but it was the book, *Learning to Be 85,* that moved me so.

The author begins her story in a little town in eastern North Carolina in a Methodist parsonage. There she lived until she was five when a major change came into her life. Oklahoma was chartered as a state in 1907, having been Indian Territory prior to this. That's where the book really begins—a parsonage home on America's frontier. Then, there begins the thrilling story of growing up, growing older, and finally growing old. But what Dr. Welch really ends up with is the finest treatise I have seen on the church's ministry to its senior citizens. When I entered the ministry, the emphasis was on youth ministries, as it still is, but a new emphasis is struggling to be born. It is the church's ministry to the aging.

I only wish that I could have read and studied this book before I arrived at the age of retirement, but it is not too late to help with the aging as well as to enjoy that aging process.

One other word—the book is fun. It will make you remember. It will cause you to laugh. It will bring tears to your eyes and will accelerate your desire to remember Robert Browning:

Grow old along with me!
The best is yet to be.

Dr. Welch's book, *Learning to Be 85,* will help it be so.

W. KENNETH GOODSON
Bishop (Ret.)
The United Methodist Church

Preface

In the week of July 18-23, 1988, middle-age America took over the stage as youth surrendered its domination of our society. For on Wednesday of that week, middle agers totaled more than seventy million, and they ushered in a new age—the Age of the Older Americans. Never before has the numerical force of the elders made available such a reservoir of talent, experience, wisdom, skills, knowledge, and attitudes. The probability that this will not happen again makes this a once-in-history occurrence. Thus, for the next century, a dimension is added to our time in history—a dimension that unites experience with numerical dominance. This combination translates into power in decision making and in policy formation.

This is a new role for older persons, and many profess a lack of readiness for the awesome responsibility facing them in areas of information and complexity of issues, especially since many of the issues will be morally and ethically based. This book deals with this quandary in the final chapters. The 1990s are a time for older persons to develop a new role of responsible leadership to replace the stereotype of "I've served my time—let someone else do it." The elders *are* it—the ones to be both doers and recipients, initiators, planners, creators. And the older woman, a majority within the older majority, will find herself the determining factor in effecting quality of life for the entire society.

To deal intelligently and pleasurably with this critical age, the elders will require learning—learning to be old, to value oldness as a precious possession, as a banner to wave and a trumpet to blow. As each of us "learned" to be five, fifteen, thirty, and sixty, we were not only *getting older,* we were *growing* as we aged. In the era ahead when it is "in" to be old, we shall find it desirable to eliminate the word *retirement* from our vocabularies, for it will not fit into the new age. "Reinvestment" creates a dynamic attitude, and making a career out of aging sets the agenda for the Age of Gerontocracy—a time when the elders of our society will have the opportunity to exercise great political power and influence because of their great numbers.

In this book I have selected certain events at certain ages that provided particular teachable moments—times when I learned, either consciously or unconsciously, important lessons that made me who I am at eighty-five. If my abilities at age five were not as advanced as those of others, then at eighty-five I might again be an underachiever or a "late bloomer," immature in relation to my chronological age. If at age five I was searching, wondering, and curious, then at eighty-five I am not fearful of the uncertainties that later years bring, and I welcome the testing of unexplored abilities as the way in which life waves me on to invigorating and challenging changes. Life even confronts me with the daring to be the catalyst for those changes that make for progress.

In the first six chapters I use a particular event and age to indicate a learning that has proved to be not only beneficial but essential to my being eighty-five. In the latter chapters I span several ages to show the cumulative effects of past events. However, it is the *event* that is memorable, and the age simply places the experience in the timeline of my life. All the learnings have brought me to this moment, and it may be that you will find some common denominators as you identify with some of your own remembrances.

In the final chapters, I will speak about my generation and its numerical impact—the ushering in of the "Age of Gerontocracy," and the geriatric echo generated by this age. Its impact presents both problems and opportunities, and a report card of both will concentrate upon the influence of this new age and its potential for unexplored and undeveloped power inherent within its experience, skills, wisdom, and expertise.

I have, on occasion, used conversation, but since there was no recording of what was said, nor anyone taking notes, it is necessary to point out that such dialogue does not in most cases represent exact words. But the dialogue does represent the gist and the spirit, as well as reflect the personalities and characteristics of those involved. I have taken care not to intentionally compromise the thrust of the matter being discussed.

Most of the names used are fictitious although the people are real. I consider the right to privacy a privilege to be highly valued and respected. I have used the real names of three of my teachers—Miss Stratton, Miss Capshaw, and Judge Hyatt—because what they did for me in their classrooms deserves my personal tribute.

I have used the Age of Gerontocracy to designate those generations who, in their numerical influence, make of the next century *their* age. I refer to these older generations as "elders" not in any sense as an official title or societal category, but as a tribute to our aging populations, to their "stayability," to their wisdom, to their commitment to what they have believed in, and to their years of experience. In their years of making a world significant to themselves and to others, these persons have earned the honor and dignity of the term *Elders*.

My life spans eighty-five years of the most cataclysmic changes in our nation's history, and, in a very real sense, I am part of that history, *being there,* often in unique situations with unusual people in places radically changed now, or erased completely by these years. Essentially, the learnings that have brought me to this age arose from where I was and the people who were a part of my world. Things that I see as so vital to making me who I am are my adaptability to change; my discovering who I was and what my identity had to do with my name; my understanding of how important a sense of humor is; my realization of the real meaning of giving; and my learning how to grow into responsibility. I must also acknowledge the power of prayer and a personal spiritual faith. Certainly I also benefitted from the unlearning of prejudice, from giving others the respect they are due, from realizing what personal relationships mean to me, and from seeing how teaching translates into being taught.

All of these things now help me see the great challenge of the aging process that brings with it a new sense of responsibility for a ''re-engagement'' with the world and for making a career out of aging.

There is still a great deal of unfinished business, but with the numerical power and the accumulated resources of these numbers, the real challenge is how older persons will use their ''hour upon the stage'' to make a mighty difference that is inherent in their great possibilities.

If I were sending a postcard to those generations following along this road, I think I would use the familiar words of the travelers: ''Having a wonderful time! Wish you were here.''

PART ONE

MY STORY: How I Learned to Be Eighty-Five

1.
At Five:
I Learn to Accept and Welcome Change

Life in a Methodist Parsonage is, in itself, a great drama, a mixture of comedy and tragedy. It has no definite beginning unless we use as a beginning each new home to which the presiding Bishop sends the minister and his family. Its plot is a series of the tragic-comic events which hourly and daily face the members of the Parsonage household. And for its end . . . there is none; once "parsonage," always "parsonage."[1]

—Sunday's Child

Born in Hope Mills, North Carolina, on August 4, 1905, I lived in eastern North Carolina my first four years, with little, if any, changes in my life. I remember a large dog whose job it was to guard me at play and to bark to let my mother know if or when I was causing him a problem. I also remember a piano and my mother holding me on her lap as she placed my small hands on the keys and pressed them gently down to create a tune that I joyfully played. I can recall an Easter with colored eggs. I can still picture a vivid blue one and baby chicks at play in a small open box. But there are only scattered recollections until our family of three experienced a great uprooting.

It was at this point that I learned to be five quickly and painlessly. Oklahoma had just been chartered as a state in 1907, having been Indian Territory and Oklahoma Territory prior to its reception into the United States of America. This pioneer state needed young ministers who could undertake the building of churches throughout the new territory—courageous ministers to serve the needs of the melting pot of a new state. The bishop of my father's Methodist Conference, along with other bishops, sent out appeals to ask young men and young families to "Go west, young man, go west!" to aid in the developing of the state's religious foundations. My father, always eager to try new experiences that tested his abilities, decided to answer the call. My father was a native of South Carolina, and my mother was born in eastern North Carolina. The most sand either had seen was the coastal dunes. And suddenly, sand was everywhere!

This abrupt change in our lives was physical, emotional, mental, social, and spiritual. It broke familiar connections and demanded, almost immediately, that we develop new relationships. The shock could have been disastrous, or it could have been a prelude to adventure. In my case, it had no undertones of disaster; what it may have been for my young father and mother, I do not know. Yet, to me, change has always seemed to open a new door with surprising things beyond—things not always enjoyable, but always filled with expectations that would be fulfilled in ways that would test my imagination and initiative. Problems in my home were normal; they were to solve, and I was not encouraged to expect ready-made answers. I recall these changes as exciting; I was filled with wonder at what was ahead.

So, at five, I went with my parents to a strange new place. Here were wide open spaces with very few trees, and all around was the yellowish grit of sand. Over everything from horizon to horizon there seemed to hang a glassy haze. The choking heat of the sandstorms that swept at all-too-frequent intervals from the Panhandle, deluged the town and its inhabitants in dry, gritty, penetrating dust. The dust crept in through the pores of the walls, through keyholes, and under doors. We would run to stuff rugs and towels into every possible crack, but still the omnipresent sand/dust was there—in our eyes, in our mouths, in our lungs. If the rains did come, they helped only temporarily, for the dry sand would suck in the drops of water as fast as they fell, and no trace of moisture would remain.

One of my earliest disappointments was the failure of my miniature garden that I tended with great care. With cups of hoarded water, I had kept a few scrubby little flowers alive in the small space my father had lined off with twine beside the house. For a little while some sweet alyssum, some mignonette, a hollyhock or two, and a pathetic morning glory vine grew there. And then, one afternoon while we were out in the country paying a pastoral call, we heard the dreaded sound of the wind from the Panhandle—no other sound was like it. The high, whining blade of its tone cut through distance from miles away and warned that it was coming. We could not get back home that evening, so we remained at the Wilkins' farm until the storm subsided. The next afternoon we could see where and how to drive back home. When we arrived, I went out to check on my flowers that had been struggling so hard to stay alive. Not one sprig of green was showing; over everything was the beige-brown cover of sand, hiding even the outlines of the six-by-eight plot. The Sand soon became a person to us, someone we dreaded—someone we knew would inevitably come again, and someone we could not shut out. It was almost as if the Wind had sworn eternal enmity against us—the invaders who had intruded into this land to wrest the present and the future. The struggle was endless, and both were unyielding, determined.

Water was scarce and, therefore, precious. Even in the tributary of one of the rare rivers water was present only in the freshets that came after cloudbursts. And we couldn't drink that, nor wade in it, nor swim in it because of the quicksands; people died when trapped in the quicksand. So, wet or dry, sand was our enemy. Sometimes, on still, hot nights, the three of us sat on the porch listening to the enveloping silence. These were the times when we talked about a lot of things. When I was five, I knew that I was a part of a family, that I could say what I wanted to say, and that my parents would really hear me.

I understood that my father and mother counted every penny they received because money was a scarce commodity in our household. The members of my father's church were hard-working people, pioneers in a pioneer state, and often my father's pay had to be in produce raised on their arid land. My mother was a wonderful cook, and what she did with the limited supplies we had seems to me, today, nothing short of a miracle.

On Saturdays, when the people would come in for their weekly shopping and to stay over for the Sunday services (many of them would sleep that night in wagons that circled the church and parsonage), there would be that wonderful camaraderie of the open plains as everyone visited and caught up on what had happened since they last met. Following the church service, everyone enjoyed a great meal and time of socializing. The food and the friendliness we looked forward to on Saturday and Sunday came to stand for the characteristic neighborliness that I have always associated with that state and its people. On some occasions, I would be invited to sleep in a covered wagon. I can hear, even now, the soft whinnying of the horses tethered just beyond the wagons, and I can see that one bright star shining through the opened flap at the rear of the wagon. And now and then, a rare and prayed-for rain would put me to sleep as the drops kept a drum-like rhythm upon the canvas top above me.

When Sunday afternoon began to slope downward into evening, the wagons would be packed, and the people would pull out in a long, snakelike line, echoing to each other, "See you next Sunday." They knew that the next week the church bell would peal out across the prairie and summon them back to the little white church. These were great people, making a greatness felt as they created a life for themselves and their children here where the struggle never ceased. And when I was five, I wanted to be like them. I was learning what it was to be in at the beginning of a state, to live among people who believed in something enough to dare their all to make it happen!

There were droughts and sandstorms—seemingly every curve nature could throw them—but they combined the grimness of determination with an all-embracing sense of humor that was an unbeatable combination. I remember late one hot afternoon the sound of a whirring and humming, coming from such a distance that, at first, it was only a whisper. But the people in the town knew what it was. And my mother knew from having been warned. This was the coming of the swarms of locusts, and they would get into every nook and cranny where there was any greenery to eat. My father came home from his study in the church, and we began to plug up all the gaps we could find in the house. This was no easy task, for crevices seemed to have been a part of the architect's plan. We had just finished this job when the sky became dark with the great clouds of locusts, bearing down implacably upon the town. We shut the door and stayed inside all night.

The next morning we looked out and saw that nothing was left of the one tree that had held on for so long but had at last surrendered to the ravenous gnawing of thousands of locusts. The three of us went out into the yard, killed whatever still crawled on the ground or swarmed up the trunk of the tree, and then swept up tubs full of dead locusts. Bonfires were being lit all over town, and, finally, all the locusts were gone. But they would come again another time. It was the reality of this and other inevitabilities that bred a stubborn determination in the people to say, "We'll be waiting." And they were, always waiting, testing their strength, often losing, but more often winning in the endless tug-of-war with nature. I learned "stayability" from them, and I also came to see what a good lubricant a sense of humor is to raw nerves.

At Conference (the area meeting held in November each year), we were moved to another town, and then to another until my father had built churches from the Panhandle of Oklahoma to Norman, where he began a church for the University of Oklahoma. He didn't get to serve this church as pastor, for another major change would send us back to our home state of North Carolina. My father joined the armed services as a chaplain in World War I and was assigned to Camp Greene in Charlotte, North Carolina. More of that later.

Before leaving Oklahoma, my father served as minister to a small remnant of Cherokee Indians who had left North Carolina on their heartbreaking "trail of tears" and had stopped off in the "garden spot" of the state. Here plenteous rainfall caused fruit trees to blossom and produce delicious peaches, plums, and cherries. It must have made this small group of Indians feel at home after having been driven from their homes in the western North Carolina mountains.

They had broken off from the larger number going on to the reservations farther west, and had made their home here. The children of the Cherokees were my first classmates and friends in my new state, and although my white skin might have made me an outsider among them, they accepted me because I was the daughter of the minster. When I was five, skin color didn't matter—only acceptance and inclusion. And at eighty-five, I find this still to be true. My father was their friend and the "Great Spirit Messenger," and our parsonage home became a refuge for them in a time of need. On many a morning, I can recall coming into the living room (we called it the parlour then), and finding some of our Indian friends sleeping there, for we left our front door open all the time. My father felt that our home must never be closed to anyone needing help—we were there as representatives of a Heavenly Father who loved everyone, and we must be reachable. My mother was more skeptical of this open-door policy. She would leave the front door unlocked, but always she had a chair propped under the doors of our upstairs bedrooms and a rolling pin close at hand for defense. She believed that although God would take care of us, God expected some cooperation from us!

The Cherokees became an integral part of my early life, when, in learning to be five and a little older, I was accepted by them as their friend and playmate. Exclusion would have meant isolation. They also taught me three important lessons: They reinforced my early feelings of the importance of family. They taught me to be proud of my origin, and through their eyes I saw the world of nature as a "thing of beauty" and "a joy forever." I believe that it was at this time that I began to accept an obligation of being a good steward of this earth and its resources, and, like the Athenians of old, of wanting to leave my surroundings better for having been here. By the age of sixty, I probably could have been called an environmentalist with a commitment to the preservation and conservation of my world.

Later in my life, I became fascinated with the story of Tsali and his kinsmen who were forced to emigrate from their native mountain homes and take the long—and agonizing—trek to the distant West, a trek called the "Trail of Tears." Some lines that I wrote from my deep consciousness of the meaning of these Native Americans to our culture and our heritage reflect an identification with them that not only lasted, but increased with the passing years.

> The laurel has covered the mountains . . .
> With carpets of pink and deep purple . . .
> The waters of Deep Creek have murmured
> The story of Tsali for many long moons.
> And the haze from the Smokies
> Mounts up to the wide skies above them . . .
> Mounts up . . . In its grey veil enfolding
> The figures of Tsali and kinsmen,
> Enfolds them to keep them . . . forever . . .
>
> They walk with the moonflower at midnight.
> They talk with the redbird at twilight.
> They sing in the cascading waters
> That sweep down the gaunt sides of Clingman . . .
>
> The race that once lived here is vanished.
> They've built in the West a new nation,
> But here stay the Cherokee people,
> And here stay the last of a nation
> Who honor the courage of Tsali . . .
> Who call him the "Great of his people!"
> His name is a symbol of freedom . . .
> His life that he gave for his people
> Lives on in the crags high on Clingman . . .
> Flows ever along Tuckaseegee . . .

A universal and poignant sadness is shared here with a people dispossessed as thousands today have been; and I, as a child, felt some of the change inherent in this sadness, though not having experienced it. I didn't yet know the grief of separation from home and lands of my origin nor the insecurity of the unknown. But at five I sensed it—and have carried it with me at eighty-five.

So, at the age of five, I knew that I was living in a new state, that it and I were growing up together, and that I was living history as it was happening. The continuity of it wrapped itself about me, and I became unconsciously a part of others, something so important to me then as a child, and, now at eighty-five, as the last surviving member of a once-large group of relatives, I face being alone without any sense of loneliness. For at five I learned that I was part of everything that had gone before me and a part of everything that ever will be; I am in the timeline of history, and it never stops. I believe that all of this began when I was learning to be five in a world of constant change. And it was normal, right, and exciting!

2.
At Seven:
Learning Expands

When I was seven, another town was our new home. It was a little larger than the one we had left, but one with a church to build and with people who had left the security of their former homes to seek a new land of opportunity.

Here the parsonage was next door to the building that was serving as the present house of worship. In this new home, I had an upstairs bedroom/playroom, and outside my window stood a locust tree where my father had hung a swing. I soared skyward in that swing as I tried to obey my mother's warnings to "be careful."

I Learn Who I Am

I did a lot of thinking as I swung back and forth, and probably it was here that my first ponderings about *me* as *me* became actual questions. I seemed to have been happy enough about myself, but, at seven, I had begun envying Blanche Baggott's long, black curls and wishing I had hair like hers. (Blanche was my best friend, and I thought she was beautiful.) I knew I was not supposed to covet anyone's possessions, but I simply could not help, to my own detriment, comparing my nondescript brown hair to her luxuriant curls. Then one day something happened, and the moment it did I knew who I was.

On that afternoon in my seventh year, I was sitting in front of my small dressing table, made for me by my father out of a discarded crate, with a drapery made by my mother from a dyed sheet. She had ruffled it—I remember—and it was beautiful. I was eyeing my image in the mirror, with my chin propped in my two hands, and what I was seeing was reflected by the frown on my face. I said to the image in the mirror, "You are ugly, and I hate what you look like!" And then I burst out, "Why can't you have hair like Blanche?" I was intensely concerned. "Why can't you look like Blanche looks?"

My mother was passing through the hall and heard me through the open door. She came up behind me, put her hands on my shoulders, leaned over me, and our eyes met in the mirror. She asked me what was bothering me, and I told her *I* was bothering me—what I looked like, especially my ugly brown hair. (I really did have curly hair, but my curls just "happened.") My mother put her face close beside mine, and her hands dropped from my shoulders, encircling me in a tight hug. A wonderful feeling came over me as our two faces side by side almost became one. After a long silence, as we looked at each other in the mirror, she said to me, "If you looked like Blanche Baggott, you'd have to be Mrs. Baggott's little girl. Would you like that?"

This was a frightening possibility, for I didn't like Mrs. Baggott very much. I said, "Not ever do I want to be Mrs. Baggott's daughter!" (I really didn't think that Blanche wanted to be Mrs. Baggott's daughter, for she had said several times that she wished she lived at my house where we had such good times together.) Then my mother hugged me even harder and said something that made me know who I was then and forever after: "You are the way you are because you belong to your father and to me. You are a part of both of us, and there is no one else in the whole world just like you. You are very special, and we love you just as you are."

From then on, I was proud of my brown hair, and I never wanted to be anyone else but myself. To deny myself would have been to deny the two people I loved most. Of course, many times through the years I compared myself with others whose appearances and lots in life I admired, but remembering my mother's face next to mine made me want to be me in my own best way. At eighty-five it is important for me to know myself as a real person, not an artificial or borrowed personality; I must not be a stranger to myself, and I must always be comfortable with the reality of who I am. If I like me, I won't mind being alone with me, nor will I shun the times of inevitable solitude when I am my only companion. This "teachable moment" at age seven has afforded me a growing sense of familiarity as other years, other experiences, and other changes, most of them unpredictable, many potentially destructive, have come into my life.

For those who are aging, the feeling of dependency and the dread of being alone top the list of losses they experience. My mother's face in the mirror gave me a lasting sense of belongingness, but dependency always puts stringent limitations on customary freedom to do, to go, to be as one wishes. Especially difficult is having to accept from others when one has always been the giver. Giving can create a habitual attitude of the power derived from giving, and it is very hard in the later years to be on the receiving end as a dependent.

Something happened much later in my life, in my twenties, that bears a close relationship to my learning to be seven. I was teaching a ninth grade English class, and a production of *The Corn Is Green,* featuring Ethel Barrymore, was coming to town. I wanted very much to see it but couldn't because the Depression and local bank failure had made theater tickets off limits for my teacher's salary, as well as for most of my students, who had difficulty finding lunch money. We talked about the play, wished we could see it, and forgot about it. Or so I thought. And then, the day before the performance, I found on my desk an envelope with a ticket in it for a seat in the fourth row. It was signed, "From your students. Go for us!"

I was deeply moved by this, but I knew how giving me that ticket had drawn on their limited money for lunch and other necessities, and I felt that I couldn't accept it. I told them in class that day how much I appreciated what they had done, but that I couldn't take the ticket, that they should return it and get their money back. A dead silence fell over the room, and we all became strangers at that moment. I had hurt them terribly by the refusal of their gift.

As I opened the door to my home after school that day, my telephone was ringing. It was one of the mothers, and her first words stunned me. "How could you turn down a gift which meant so much to the children in the giving of it? They wanted you to have the ticket, and they enjoyed going without whatever it took to get it. Don't you understand how to *receive* from others as well as to give to them? You cheated them today of their joy in planning and giving you this surprise, and you cheated yourself in being a gracious receiver."

I thanked her for pointing out a valuable lesson I needed to learn and told her that I would accept the ticket. The next day I walked to the front of the room and thanked my students for the ticket, telling them I would indeed go and have a wonderful time. Smiles replaced the grim looks with which the students had greeted me at the start of the class. I had learned a very important lesson. My earliest years had made me a receiver more often than a giver, and at age eighty-five, it is necessary to be a gracious receiver as well as a benefactor. It isn't always easy, for independence, so essential in reaching selfhood, becomes a precious possession to treasure as long as we have breath.

I Learn to Respect Others' Property

At age seven I also learned a valuable lesson about my responsibility to others and for things that did not belong to me. From my earliest years I had always known that I was to respect what other people owned. While sharing with others was a principle to be adhered to, taking from them or abusing what they owned was a "no-no." But there was a gray area that I had never had to consider, related to property only temporarily mine, such as the parsonage in which I lived. My playroom was mine for the time we lived in this home, but it would be someone else's when we left, and it must be left in good condition for the next inhabitant. I knew this and agreed with it. I took good care of my room and was proud of its appearance.

One Sunday morning, I put on my white organdy dress (which I disliked because I considered it so uninteresting; however, white organdy served so many purposes for me that it was always my "best dress"). I went to Sunday school that morning, and later in the service a visiting minister spoke about foreign missions and urged that we learn everything we could about these countries where the "heathen" needed our help. He had a lot of printed pamphlets, about four inches wide and ten inches long in various bright colors. These gave additional facts about the different countries where our money would go. When the services were over and all had left, I asked my father if I might take some of the pamphlets with me and read them that afternoon. He thought it was a good idea and told me to help myself to what were left. I carried an armful of them home, and after the noontime dinner, I went to my playroom and seated all of my dolls in a semicircle facing one wall of the playroom, newly calcimined in robin's-egg blue. I had always liked the color of the room before this event, but since that day, I have a strong aversion to it.

After seating the dolls in the best positions for their attention, I began pasting the pamphlets, one by one, around the wall at eye level so that all of us could read. I used flour paste, and a blob of paste held each pamphlet in almost a complete circle around the walls. I talked to my "congregation" about the pamphlets and the need for them to do their duty. At the end of the "service," I seem to have felt good about what I had done—I felt that I had done what the speaker that morning had asked us to do. At any rate, I do not remember having had any sense of doing wrong. But after putting my dolls away, I began removing the pamphlets so as to leave the room in good order. I still recall the awful sinking feeling I had when I pulled the first pamphlet from the wall. Most of the pamphlet came away, but where the blob of paste had held it to the wall, either the paper still stuck in big pieces or the calcimine came away with the paper. In a circle all around the room, at my eye level, were pieces of paper or peeled spots making a polka-dot design. I stood there horrified, unable to cry or to speak, knowing very well that calamity had struck. After a while and after somewhat recovering from the shock, I faced up to telling my parents about it; for even if I had thought that this could be kept from them, those thirty or forty spots on the wall told the story. Besides, I had never been afraid to tell my parents what I had done; it was just that this time I seemed to have pulled a real whopper!

I slowly went downstairs and found my mother in the parlour, reading. My father was over at the church preparing for a meeting of the official board in the late afternoon. I stood looking at my mother, and when she looked up, she must have known that a catastrophe had occurred. She asked what was the matter, and, hesitatingly, I told her she'd have to see it to believe it. We started upstairs, and I told her that I had been "educating" my dolls and had put pamphlets on the walls, but the pamphlets wouldn't come off . . . that is, not completely. I hadn't meant to ruin the walls.

We opened the door together, went in, and she just looked around the room—slowly and deliberately. She didn't say a word. Finally she sat down in a chair, pulled me to her, put her arm around me, and said, "You know, we'll have to pay to have this room done over. It will cost about twenty-five dollars, and we don't have the money. What do you think we can do?"

I didn't have any answer. I was overwhelmed at what I had done, and she knew it. "We'll wait until your father comes home, and then we'll decide." In the meantime, I was to stay in the room and think! In that robin's-egg blue room, my thoughts were quite dark!

When my father came in from the church, my mother told him to come upstairs to the playroom where I was waiting. He, of course, had no way of knowing what to expect, but when he walked in, he, too, stood silently, just looking around at the blobs on the wall. He motioned to my mother to come with him downstairs, but he told me to wait there by myself in the playroom until he called.

After what seemed to me like an eternity, he called me to join him and my mother downstairs, and, there, as a family, we decided what to do next. Of course the room had to be recalcimined, and the money for that would require us to do without some necessities. One of these sacrifices was to be my small allowance, and I made no objection. (Although this meant very little in the total twenty-five dollars, it was my part of the restitution—two cents a week!) My parents suggested that I go out and play while they did some figuring. No word of punishment was mentioned. I asked them what they were going to do to me for what I had done, and their answer was, "Nothing at this moment." They both knew I had not meant to do anything wrong, so there was no intentional act. Perhaps they thought that I had been punished enough. At any rate, I went out to swing and to let this new lesson be learned—never, never, never do anything to anybody else's property. To this day, I will not drive anyone else's car, wear anybody else's clothes, drive a nail in the wall of any rented dwelling without specific permission, or borrow anything without ensuring that the lender approves and that a return time is set. That robin's-egg blue is a perpetual alarm system.

The ending was a happy one. That afternoon when the official board met, my father reported to them the damage to the newly-painted playroom. They wanted to know what happened, and my father said I was the one to tell them about it. He came home across the yard between our house and the church and asked my mother to bring me over in a little while when he motioned from the door. She dressed me in the white organdy and, holding my hand closely, she walked across to the church when my father waved to us. As we reached the building, she turned back home, and I went on alone to where my father waited for me. He took my hand, led me inside the building, and I recall the awesomeness of that assembly of officials of the church, sitting there in two rows, eyeing me. On only one face did I seem to see the faint tracing of a smile, and, later, as I explained, this person openly grinned and appeared to be thoroughly enjoying the experience. My father presented me to the board, said I had something to say, and then left it to me. I was probably short of breath and scared to death, but it was my doing, and I had to take care of it. I explained that I had thought my dolls needed to be informed about the foreign missions and that I had had a service for them and had pasted the pamphlets on the wall without even thinking that I couldn't remove them when we were finished. But the paper had stuck to the calcimine, and the walls had large pieces of paper stuck around and pieces of the calcimine had pulled away when the paper came off. I didn't attempt to plead with them; I said I didn't mean to damage the wall, and that I thought I was doing what the man in the morning service asked us to do. When I finished, my father asked if they wanted to ask me anything; nobody spoke, and my father said I could leave, but I was to wait for him at home until he came. I left, with the smile of one of the men affording me some degree of comfort.

When my father came, he and my mother talked for a short time, and then they asked me to join the family council. My father said that the board had discussed what I had done, that they didn't believe that I had intended any harm, that they were sure I'd learned my lesson, and that since I was going to contribute two cents a week for six months, they would make up the difference and pay for calcimining the room again! My father and mother were more than happy about the result. My only comment was that I hoped the color would not be robin's-egg blue. (It wasn't. They let me choose the shade, and I chose a pale yellow!) So the age of seven taught me that what was mine, was mine to share with others, but what was theirs, was theirs to keep until they chose to let me share with them.

I Learn to Make Music

At seven, a new world opened for me. This was the world of music; the music *I* made. Ever since my mother had held me on her lap while she practiced her music—she had a beautiful soprano voice and was a fine musician—I had been almost hypnotized by the sounds of music, and the piano was a magnet that attracted me away from any toys with which I might be playing. I would toddle over to the upright piano every chance I got, hold on to the edge of it, and press whatever keys I could reach. It seemed that I knew when a key was right, and sometimes I would even put several keys together to make a tune.

My mother noticed that I could repeat what she had just played, and she felt that I had a real ear for music. But she never pressured me to practice or to work at it. She taught me the scales and led me to the "arithmetic" of music—the notes and their values, the meaning of key signatures, and how each measure equaled the time indicated for that part of the music—but she waited for me to let her know when I was ready for formal study of music. When I was seven, she knew the time was right. I was beginning to create tunes of my own, and I could play much of what she played by ear, but she believed I must soon understand the discipline of playing by note, of reading music. So she and my father asked Miss Miriam Landrum, the daughter of our doctor and a trained musician, to visit with us one afternoon and let us know what she thought. They hoped that she would agree to take me on as a pupil, for she was an excellent teacher.

She asked me to play something for her, which I did, but I played it *my* way, which was not the way it was written. She asked me to play it the way it was written, and I did the best I could; but then I played it again in another key, this time the way I heard it. She was surprised, and said she thought it would be interesting having me as a pupil. She said she was sure we would have unusual times together. She was right. She was a demanding teacher and a tough taskmistress, but my music lessons became the calendar event of each week for me.

My mother had warned her never to play any new piece for me before being sure that I could play it by note, because playing by ear was so easy after I heard a piece of music that I might never bother to learn to read the notes. Bless her, she caught on quickly, and she disciplined me to the rigors of sightreading and of playing the music as it was written. But after I had done this, I would play that same music in many other keys just for fun. I thoroughly enjoyed repeating what I heard others sing or play, changing it into a pattern all my own. I am frequently asked today how I do this, and my honest answer is that I don't know—I just do it and I seem always to have been able to do it. It is a great help to me now when I play for our Sharps and Flats band, or when I play for singalongs, for choirs, for church meetings, for club programs, or for group singing anywhere to be able to transpose music into keys where it is comfortable for people to sing. (I often think it is so unfortunate that music seems to have been written as if the only ones to sing it are trained vocalists. Medium keys are more adaptable for the ordinary singer who just wants to enjoy singing with others.)

My father, too, was musical and enjoyed nothing more than leading a congregation in zestful singing (which was usually easier to join than was the mournful and off-key singing of the choir). When my father led the singing, the people sang the roof off with real abandon and self-involvement. At home, almost every evening after supper our family of three would gather at the piano for half an hour of music, whatever our fancy dictated at the moment. A few years later in my life, a little black cocker spaniel, Happy, joined our family as a gift from a lady in the congregation, and, believe it or not, she soon became a fourth in our nightly song fests. My father said that music must be contagious, for it wasn't long after she joined us that she took her place by the piano every evening, waiting for us to start. She had her favorites, apparently, for her behavior showed us clearly when she was pleased. She almost "sang" on key, howling sometimes, sometimes barking staccato accompaniments, and every once in a while, an obligato.

Happy was fatally injured while chasing another dog across a busy road, and her death created an emptiness and a sense of desolation that can be understood only by those who suffer this loss. There may be a "dog heaven," I don't know or care; but I hope that Happy will have sniffed her way to wherever my Heaven may be, and that her bark welcomes me home. I hope that her bark is an obligato to the music of the angelic choir as all of Heaven sings with Happy.

She was a member of our family, and all of us revelled in the sounds of music and made a joyful noise every chance we had. For that, I am thankful every day of my life, for music is not only a personal involvement for me, but it is a language of communication with others.

In the late 1960s I saw this kind of communication happening when I was on a seminar with a group of educators in the Soviet Union. On one of the Sundays, we asked if we might attend a church service. At that time, requests such as this were not looked upon favorably. However, we were allowed to go and were given a choice: we could attend a Baptist church service or a Catholic Mass.

Most of us, being Protestants, chose the Baptist church. About two thousand worshipers had gathered, most of them in work clothes, for this was a work day, and they would go back to their jobs after the service. Only half the people could be seated, so others stood until the service was half over. Then those seated exchanged places with those standing.

Our group was seated in the balcony. We couldn't understand the words of the speakers, but when the great organ and the voices of the choir began their magnificent anthem, we all became a part of the service. To our great amazement, the tune was familiar to all of us. We recognized it as the old hymn, "The Little Brown Church in the Vale." Unintelligible words separated us, but the familiar tune joined us as one. It may not have been the same hymn to the congregation, but it was familiar to us. We nodded to each other and began to sing in English. Soon, those on the floor below us heard us. They turned to look upward at us, to smile at us, to wave, to throw kisses to us, and some even wept in their feeling of identification with us. The singing increased in volume, and in elation, it bound us all together. At that moment, the walls of that Russian church fell away, and we were in the church universal. Music unified us in spirit that Sunday morning.

Now, at eighty-five, I am grateful to my parents and to those teachers who, enveloping me in a musical environment from infancy without any pressure to measure up to any expectations of theirs, took me where I was and taught me how to go ahead at my own pace in my own way.

At seven, the door to music opened to me, and it widens even more with each experience. It is a door, opened by my parents and opened even wider by those teachers who shared with me their talents, their great patience, and their encouragement. That door has stayed open through my own absorption with the musical experience. At eighty-five, my partial hearing loss and my two hearing aids affect the reception of words in high tones, especially from some speakers who mumble or talk too fast, but my hearing and enjoyment of music is unimpaired. I have been able to be a part of Maui native songs, Indian chants and their drum music, European folk festivals, great arias of opera, lilting tunes of Broadway musicals, the great music of Irving Berlin, and many, many other people and their music. It has been a bond between us while I was with them and long after we had parted. The one group with whom I cannot identify in this way is the rock music element. My hearing aids amplify only the noise, and I am deafened by the dissonant sounds and the great noises of this type of music. I wish it were not so, for in today's world this music speaks loudly and boldly to so many people with whom I'd like to join. Yet I am estranged when this music is played. It is not that I do not like it— it is just that, aurally, I cannot receive it without being deafened.

But the door of music has stayed open, and it is a door that never closes. For that I am truly grateful.

3.
At Nine:
I Learn to Seize the Opportunity

Whenever we moved to a new town, as we did when I was nine, the second thing my parents did was to get acquainted with its people. My father would walk down the main street of the town, go into every store, and introduce himself to everyone there, inviting them to church on Sunday. He always began this ritual after helping my mother and me unpack.

The main street of our new hometown in the Oklahoma Panhandle had buildings on each side of a deeply rutted, potholed road with the stores built right up to the plank sidewalks. There was a dry goods store, a general store for foodstuffs and the mail, a drug store, a blacksmith's shop on the corner, and, in the very center of the line of stores, there was the Laughing Mule Saloon, owned by Dallas Eicherhorn, who had come west from Pennsylvania. The saloon had a "watcher" across the street from its swinging doors—a member of the W.C.T.U. (Women's Christian Temperance Union). Today she'd be called a "picketer." My father visited in all the other stores, and finally reached the doors of the saloon. As tall as he was, he could see over the top of the doors, and his feet and legs showed below. The doors swung inward and outward to allow for quick and easy entrance and exit.

My father stood at the doors, smiled and spoke to all the men lined up along the bar, told them he was the new preacher at the Methodist Church, and invited them to come to church the next Sunday. Mr. Eicherhorn, equally genial, walked to the door and invited my father to come in. When my father courteously refused, the invitation to church was again extended to the saloon keeper. Mr. Eicherhorn smilingly answered, "Preacher, I'll come to your house when you come to mine." They shook hands and parted.

To travel over the sand and the few roads that led to the scattered homes of his congregation, my father needed transportation. He had purchased two white horses to pull the buggy in which we traveled everywhere we went, and things went well until some pranksters managed one night to get those horses up on top of the little barn. How they did this no one could ever figure out, but when my father went out to feed the animals before starting the day's itinerary, he found the horses literally frozen into a position from which they would not move. How to get them down was the pressing question, and I was sent to the next-door neighbor for help.

The whole family came after having gotten word out to others that the preacher had two horses on top of the barn and needed help to get them down. Soon practically the whole town was in our back yard, offering suggestions, but mostly laughing and making some rather pointed remarks. My mother, bless her, was standing by the barn, softly singing to calm the petrified horses, and it did seem to do some good.

Some of the men came up with the idea of lifting off first one horse and then the other by fitting a sling underneath them. Five of the strongest men would go on the roof to lower the horse until those on the ground could steady the animal as it reached safety. The horses gave no trouble for they were stiff with fright. As a matter of fact, from that time on, these horses were neurotic and could never be driven again. A few days later, one of the ranchers offered to take them out to his open land where they could run free. From that time on, the story of the horses on the roof became a town legend. The people said that they had often been to a house or barn raisin', but this was their first horse lowerin'!

Then other means of transportation had to be found—and quickly—so that my father could carry on his pastoral duties. He decided to get a motorcycle (over my mother's strong objections), and he finally located one at a knockdown price. Motorcycles were relatively scarce at the time, but by the early 1900s they had developed into useful vehicles. This machine would take my father where he needed to go—through the sand or down rutted roads—where there were roads. Of course, there was the problem of his long legs and his long coattails flying in the wind, and both might get entangled in the wheels, but he soon became adept at managing the motorcycle, and he was a careful driver. On rare occasions, he would take me for short jaunts as I held on around his waist, but only with my mother's grudging permission. Soon, traveling by motorcycle was just an everyday occurrence—until the day when I learned more about being nine.

My father was going out to a small farm where he knew I could see a newly-born calf, and he asked me if I wanted to hang on. We started off with much snorting and puffing of the machine; and with me holding on for dear life, we rode down the main street, nodding to people along the way. Then, without warning, and with no fault of my father's, the front wheel caught in the deep pothole directly in front of the Laughing Mule Saloon. The motorcycle went over on its side, throwing me off to the left where the W.C.T.U. watcher caught me and checked to see if I was hurt; I wasn't—only scared. My father sailed off to the right into the saloon, sliding on his back under the swinging door, landing at the foot of the bar. All the men standing along the bar stared down in surprise at seeing the preacher lying there, stretched out, looking up at them; they raised their glasses to him in greeting. Mr. Eicherhorn quickly came to help my father get up off the floor, brushed him off, handed him his glasses, and asked if he was hurt. He winked at Mr. Eicherhorn and the men, and then, with a wide grin and a twinkle in his eye, said, "Well, Mr. Eicherhorn, I've come to your house, now you come to mine." Then my father waved at the men and went out the swinging doors to collect me and the motorcycle, both unharmed.

The next Sunday morning our church was filled, and a lot of those present were not Methodists, for the word had gotten around that Dallas Eicherhorn would keep his word. Just as my father was leading the first hymn, "Rescue the Perishing," the doors in the rear opened, and in came not only Dallas Eicherhorn, but five of the patrons from the bar. They all slowly walked down the aisle as my father motioned them to the front pew, which, for some reason, had been left unoccupied that morning. The men sat down when the hymn was over, and soon the collection plate was passed. When it was handed to one of the men, my father motioned to him to put his gun in the plate, and, one by one, they deposited their guns that they habitually wore. At the end of the service, they collected the guns as they left. Dallas Eicherhorn joined the church a few months later, and he claimed that his reason for doing so was because the "backsliding" preacher knew how to honor a deal.

I Learn the Possibility of Loss

When I was nine, I contracted the dreaded childhood disease of that time—diphtheria. I probably would have died had I not, a few months earlier, had my tonsils out. The doctor told my parents that it was a blessing that I had had that operation. I remember that the operation was performed on our dining room table with a bright light shining down on me. The room was dark except for that overhead light. I began to feel sleepy, the talk about the room faded ever and ever so faintly away, and, suddenly, that was it! There were no hospitals for miles around, and doctors operated wherever the best conditions were, often in the home.

Later on, when my mother had to have a serious operation, this same dining room table served again. I recall how much more frightened I was about my mother's ordeal than I had been about my own, and rightfully so. The day of her operation, I was taken to a neighbor's house to spend the day. During the morning when the neighbor took me with her to the store, we passed our house, and all the window curtains were drawn. The windows looked to me like "blind eyes," and nothing seemed alive around the house. I felt alone, knowing that something strange was happening but not knowing what—and I was afraid. My mother had told me not to worry about anything, and I believed her; but even today, the image of that still, "blind" house persists in my memory.

When I was taken home late that afternoon, my father met me at the front door, hugged me, and said my mother wanted to speak to me for a minute. So, at nine-and-a-half I learned to face the possibility of loss, and I knew the feeling of loneliness, of being left behind.

To help my mother recuperate, Grace came to live with us, to wait on my mother and to take care of my father and me. She was a strong, handsome woman in her thirties, without a family of her own, and she soon belonged to us and we to her. She loved us devotedly and what she did for us could not be valued in money. Her laugh was contagious and she was a genuine friend and loving companion to me. Grace was not afraid of anything, and out here where so many strange things were happening, she was a constant source of comfort to my mother as she slowly recovered and began to assume more of her normal activity. Grace's confidence was boundless, and her optimism limitless.

I Learn to Respect Nature

I had a birthday coming up, and Grace and my mother planned a wonderful affair for me with all the children from my grade at school as my guests. Their mothers had been asked to bring the children and to stay throughout the party, not only for a visit with my mother and each other, but so they would be there to take the children home. Some of them had driven in from some distance, and they would be late getting back to their homes. The party started right after lunch, and would end about four o'clock.

Grace had made the birthday cake. The children arrived, bringing presents that I placed on a table by the large window looking westward toward the open plains outside the town. We had the refreshments, and I was beginning to open the presents when I looked up and out of the window. There in the distance were ugly, mustard-colored clouds that looked like an umbrella over the plains. Whirling and spinning out of the clouds was a huge grayish-black funnel, wide at the top and then narrowing like an elephant's trunk twisting down to the ground. It was jerking as if it were trying to pull loose from its anchor somewhere in the dust near the ground. I called out, pointing, and Grace came running to look where I was pointing. She yelled, "cyclone!" and the mothers began grabbing their children and running to their buggies and wagons to outrun the storm. Grace helped my mother into our storm cellar that was just beside the house at the kitchen steps. I grabbed one of my presents, a heart-shaped locket, just as Grace came back and pulled me in to join my mother in the cellar. Grace pushed me down the six steps to where my mother was waiting. Then she pulled the heavy double wooden doors together over our heads, and put a heavy bar across to keep the wind from tearing them off and leaving us unprotected.

I had been down in the storm cellar many times because we stored our canned goods there where it was cool. We always kept in the cellar a lantern with some fuel, some matches in a tin box, and plenty of bedclothing for the cots where we would sleep if a storm lasted all night. Every morning a bucket of fresh water would be placed on a shelf in the cellar in case we would need it that day.

The cellar was just a hollowed out, deep pit in the hard, red earth, with the two wooden doors fitted to close the only opening. On top of a small vent in the roof that let in fresh air was a tin hat that prevented water from pouring in when the rains came with the storm. Shut up in this subterranean refuge, we could hear little of the storm, but the whining, shrieking gusting of the winds gained in fury when amplified by the narrow vent above our heads.

I had a feeling of being buried inside the cellar, and the sounds of the storm didn't help. But my mother, who feared storms herself, held my hand and sang until I went to sleep, and Grace could tell the greatest stories to make me forget what was happening outside. Her stories were fascinating—if unbelievable. She told of tarantulas biting her, of crocodiles attacking her in a river, and of other weird experiences where she always won out over any dangers that beset her.

The one thing I feared most was the presence of spiders that found the storm cellar a perfect nesting spot, especially in the folds of the blankets that we kept in the cellar. But after every storm we swept down the walls and took the bed clothing up into the fresh air. Apparently we prevented spider problems, for we never were bitten by any insect in the storm cellar. Daily airing of the cellar kept it in good condition. The outhouses were another matter, for spiders and, sometimes, snakes inhabited these bathroom facilities; but we tried to be careful when using them, and most of the time, we had little trouble.

My birthday cyclone jumped over the town, but followed behind a train that outran it, so the story went. Some passengers later described the frightening pursuit by the funnel as it ripped up the track almost to the rear platform of the last coach. Then they said it gave one convulsive jerk and disintegrated within the yellow clouds around it.

My father arrived home about noon, having stayed with a member of his congregation overnight out of reach of the storm. He had worried about us but found us safe and our house untouched. Others in the more direct path of the storm had not been so fortunate, however. We knew that storms were inevitable out there, but we never quite got used to the devastation they wreaked. At nine, I learned, however, to respect nature's ferocity while enjoying her beauty. There was order in our universe, and I came to understand this, even if not accepting it with equanimity.

When we came up from the storm cellar the morning after the storm, there, beside the top step was the gift I'd been holding in my hand the night before—the gold locket with the imitation pearl in its center. The water beating on it all night had loosened the pearl, and it fell out when I picked up the locket. All my other gifts were still on the table in the dining room, and later that day, our family celebrated my birthday with more than just the usual wishes and singing—there was genuine thankfulness for our having come through the ordeal, alive and unharmed.

I Change My Name

In the fall my grandmother in North Carolina died, and my mother and I returned for her funeral. We stayed in North Carolina for a month. My grandmother and I had been very close—she at one end of the age cycle, I at the other. We spanned the distance perfectly, and my fondest early memories had been of those times, before we left for Oklahoma, when I visited in the home place where she, as an invalid for her final years, was the center of a very large and loving family of thirteen children—two girls and eleven boys. I, as the youngest grandchild, had always been welcome to sit on her big bed, listen to stories she would tell about the family, and share her breakfast tray with her, for there were special tidbits on there for me. She was a beautiful person, and we all adored her. After we went to Oklahoma, we were too far away to see her very often, and we didn't have the money to visit her every year, but we wrote to each other. Then one night a telegram came from my uncle. My grandmother had died in her sleep that morning, and they would hold the funeral services as soon as we could get there. My father couldn't get away at that time, but my mother and I took a long train trip of two and a half days on our own. For my mother, it must have been especially hard, for not only her grief at losing her mother had overwhelmed her, but her recent operation and the responsibility of looking after me on such a tiring trip placed a heavy strain upon her.

But she made the trip a wonderful educational experience for me. She turned it into a geography lesson, telling me about the places through which the train was traveling, and, once in a while, she would sing to me something that related to what we were seeing—a river, a special town, a mountain range. And on our last night, she waked me so that I could see, from the window of our berth, the broad, moonlit waters of the Mississippi River. I have a clear picture of that scene to this day, for part of it was the thought that only a very fragile railing kept our train from toppling into those waters below. I recall how slowly we were traveling, and this had been the case throughout the two-and-a-half day journey. Heavy flooding in places had required changes in schedule and creeping paces across trestles, weakened by the whirling waters. In one instance—it was at night, for I remember the lanterns of those helping us to change from one train to another—a track over a deep gorge was so weakened that the train stopped on one side of a steep chasm, and we were all told to get off. We descended steep ladders, crossed the rocky stream by a temporary wooden bridge, and climbed up on the other side by ladders to a train waiting to take us on. I was carried up and down the ladders by the conductor in our Pullman car, and another passenger helped my mother. Essential luggage was swung down and up on long ropes. Nature had gained my respect again!

All my uncles had worked throughout their lives for the Atlantic Coast Line Railroad, and several of them were in high administrative positions. One of them was in charge of transportation in the area through which we were traveling. So when our second train pulled into the next station, there he was to take care of us from then on. What a relief to my mother, for the two days since leaving Oklahoma had been strenuous and often frightening times. My uncle had been informed about the washouts of the bridges, and had come, partly to inspect the trouble, but, I'm sure, mostly to take over the shepherding of his sister and niece safely to their destination.

In the two days on the train, my mother had talked with me about my grandmother's death, and I hadn't known what to ask; it was all so strange, so final, so complete. I knew that I wasn't going to see my grandmother again as I had been seeing her, but where had she gone? My mother, in her special way, knew how to replace my sense of loss with my knowledge of the love that my grandmother and I had shared, and that would always be part of my life. I suppose that out of this first experience came my understanding of the transience of life here, and my puzzled wondering about what happened next. I suppose it was about this time that I began to develop my own personal religious beliefs, based partly in events of death among my family and friends through the years, and partly because of my life in a Methodist parsonage where a spiritual heritage was a valued gift from my parents.

We stayed a month in the home place, and then my father needed us to come back. On the day before we were to leave, there was a family gathering of all the relatives in the living room. At this time my grandmother's papers were opened, and the will was read. My mother told me about it later. The will wasn't about money, but about intangibles money can't buy. And there was a gift for me. My mother gave it to me as soon as we got back to Oklahoma. I knew about it before that, but she had kept it for fear that I might lose it before I reached home. On our first night in our own home with my mother and father looking on, I opened the little box, labeled in my grandmother's spidery handwriting: "To my beloved grandchild—I shall never be away from you, and I love you." Inside, was a small gold locket with a turquoise inset—a real one—and engraved on the back, "My love."

I had forgotten that I had written to tell her about how I lost the birthday "pearl" when I dropped the locket in the cyclone, and she must have had this one bought to send me, and never had the time. So here it was, a perpetual reminder of a beautiful lady whose love I had shared and whose name I bore as my middle name.

My name became a matter of importance. I wanted her name to be mine. I wanted to be called by her name, not the name I had been called since birth. I had asked my mother several times why she gave me my first name, and she said she was reading a book at the time I was born, and she liked the name of the little girl in the story. She hoped I'd be a girl like the storybook character. I had never been especially fond of my name, but I had never thought about it very much—until then. Since my middle name was the name of my grandmother, I decided that I would be "Elizabeth" from then on. Holding the locket in my hand, I informed my parents of my decision. I felt that what I was doing was right. They were stunned, I am sure, but they asked me why I wanted to change my name after all these years—nine of them! I said that I wanted to think it over for a little while, but I knew that I wanted to be called after my grandmother. Her name of "Elizabeth" meant something to me, but the other name—the one I'd been called—was a name from a storybook, and it didn't have any real meaning for me. I guess that, subconsciously, I was remembering my mother's face beside mine in the mirror, and I was seeking both identification and identity with my family.

At breakfast the next morning, I told them it was final—from that moment on, I was "Elizabeth." They didn't object, but they probably were amused at my declaration of independence. The problem was that my parents, out of habit, kept on calling me by my first name. I knew there was only one way to break them of this, and I addressed this difficulty at dinner one evening. After dessert, I said there was something we had to straighten out right away. I explained that since they weren't remembering to use my new name, they probably never would unless we resorted to drastic measures; from then on, I would not answer to my first name again when they called until they had called me three times. I wasn't being disobedient, nor did I want to scare them when I didn't come or answer, but if I waited for the third call, they wouldn't have time to get really worried, and, by that time, they would remember to call me Elizabeth. When they did, I would come immediately. It worked! Within a month, my new name was automatic, and I have been Elizabeth ever since. My parents liked my new name, and I felt a new sense of belonging to those I loved.

I Learn to Give

Christmas was always a memorable time in our home. We never had much money for gifts, but we found ways to make them unusual and special for the receiver. Early on, our family had established a custom, unique to us, so far as I knew. Each of us always gave away one gift and put it on the church Christmas tree on Christmas Eve. The gift we gave away was one given to us by one of the other immediate family members—never one from outside, and we would not know what the gift was before we chose it as our gift for the tree. A gift was not something to get rid of, nor a duty present; it was something to give happiness to someone. Thus, on the day before Christmas, we would put all of our presents around the tree, and, although we would not open *our* gifts until Christmas morning, we opened one gift that we each chose to give away, and then, having opened it to be sure that it was a really nice present, we would rewrap it for the church tree.

One year my mother had made a very special gift for me. I had wanted a bride doll, and I hoped I would get it that year. My mother, a gifted seamstress, had gotten some white kid leather and had made the body of the doll in separate parts so that each was moveable. The head was porcelain and handpainted, and the hair was genuine hair in curls. She dressed the doll exquisitely with handmade clothes and a long white veil. On the evening when we were to choose our present to give away, we looked at all the packages under the tree, and I chose the one wrapped in dark brown wrapping paper as my gift for the church tree. My father and mother both gasped, and my father asked, "Are you sure this is the one you want to give away?" I began to have doubts because of the way they were looking at me, but having chosen, I thought I should stick by my choice. I nodded yes and then I opened the brown-wrapped package. My heart broke in two!

There was my beautiful bride doll, a work of art made by my mother with such loving thoughtfulness. But I had chosen, and our custom was not to change once the choice was made. My parents thought I should have a second chance, and my mother was almost in tears. But as I rewrapped the doll in Christmas paper and ribbons, and when the time came to go over to the church and put our gifts on the tree, every step I took was as if I were rooted to the ground. I finally reached the church, and hesitantly, I walked down the aisle and handed my package to the people loading the tree. Little did they know that I was giving my heart away. They put my gift toward the top of the tree, and all through the service, my eyes were on it. I could still renege and take it back, but it really wasn't mine to own anymore—I had given it away.

Then came the time to give out the presents. It seemed they'd never get to the doll; but at last, with only one present left, the number for my present was called. No one claimed the number. I felt a surge of hope, for maybe, just maybe no one would go up for it, and I could have it after all. But just then I heard a dragging step passing the pew where I sat, and I turned to see who was going to receive the doll. It was a small girl in rather worn clothing, and her slowness in walking was because she was on crutches. I did not recognize her, but apparently she was someone from the poorest section of the town who did not attend regular church services.

When she reached the chancel rail and braced herself against it, Santa Claus handed her the package. She tried to take it, but her crutches prevented her from holding it. Santa Claus unwrapped the package and gave her the doll. The whole congregation went "Ah-h-h!" when the doll was held up, and the little girl cried out as if she had no words. My mother was looking at me, and she reached out to hold me in a tight hug. I was crying.

Then the little girl reached out her arms, and Santa Claus placed the doll in them. She hugged the doll tightly to her and asked, "It's mine? It's really mine?" Santa nodded and she turned to go back to her seat. Her face was simply radiant, and at that moment, I really gave her my doll. It wasn't mine any longer, and, to my surprise, I wasn't sad about it. Without understanding at all what had happened to me, I knew that only by giving away the doll would I have it forever. And the doll is still mine.

My mother said to me the next day that she would make me another bride doll, but I refused it, because having given it away I had really kept it, and I didn't need two. At eighty-five, that moment holds a very special place in my life.

4.
At Twelve:
Prayer and a Pink Dress

As a P.K. (Preacher's Kid), I accepted as natural and normal many things that seemed extraordinary to others of my age. For instance, a pink dress was not unusual for my girl friends, but for me, a pink dress was something to yearn for, to dream about, to pray for, but not to expect too hopefully. My best dress was always a white organdy because it served for any and all occasions: church, parties, weddings, and funerals. But as I remarked to my father on one occasion, "It's too bad God dressed all his angels in white. They'd look so much more heavenly in pink." My father smiled at me, but was puzzled as he so often was by things I said. He left matters of clothing entirely to my mother who was an expert at so many things like sewing. There was no money in the parsonage for pink dresses, and we all knew it.

There was to be a very important party at "The Clubhouse" (the scene of most of the social events in the town, and for us in the parsonage, many of these events were off limits). This party was to honor a brother and sister who were my classmates at school, and their parents were members of our church. All of my school friends were going, and my parents thought I should go—they just wanted to take precautions about the preacher letting his daughter go to such a "den of iniquity." I was filled with anticipation.

I had not been allowed to date anyone up until then, for my parents felt that I was too young to become emotionally involved with one boy. This had never bothered me, for I had a good time with all my classmates. But there was one boy I liked a lot, and I helped him with his Latin when he asked me—which was fairly often. He needed a little encouragement to ask me to go with him to the party, but he finally got around to it. After a short delay, I accepted. Then my agony began, for I didn't want to wear that white organdy dress to the party. I decided that this matter needed a family council meeting.

After dinner a week before the party, we stayed at the dinner table for a conference, and I broached the question: "Is there any way in which I could have a new dress for the party? A pink dress? There's just the material down at the dry goods store, and it's beautiful!" My parents looked at each other, and, sadly, shook their heads negatively.

"Not unless somebody decides to get married," said my father. "Then, whatever the groom gives me for marrying them, I'd turn over to your mother. But right now, there's no sign of any wedding."

My mother remarked that if Mrs. Askew didn't have a heart attack every time Amelia mentioned marrying Ben Tedrow, there was the perfect couple. "And Ben's been waiting for years, and Amelia just won't risk being the cause of her mother's death. So he just waits."

During this entire conversation, we had hardly noticed that Chief Green Feather, one of our Indian friends, had been sitting in the corner, quietly listening and smoking his pipe. At this point, he got up, raised his hand in farewell, and left. We didn't think anything of it because he and others from his tribe often came in, sat down, and went away when they wanted to. At first this had troubled my mother—this coming in and sitting, listening—but my father had reassured her, saying that they felt safe here, and they were always welcomed.

So this time, none of us paid any attention to his having been there, and we forgot that he had sat through the whole conversation. We got back to the dress I wanted, and tried rebalancing the budget, but there just wasn't the money for the dress. Each day I would walk by the dry goods store to see if the pink *mousseline de soie* material was still in the window. Time was short, and no one seemed headed for the altar. My mother was worried about it, and my father was encouraging me every day not to give up hope, to keep on praying for the dress.

I finally decided it was time for me to put it up to God. We had done all we could, and now I would have to remind God that I had reached my limits of effort, and it was up to him. My prayer was very personal—I spoke just as I would have presented my case to my father. I quote here from *Sunday's Child,* the dramatized version of this incident that I wrote:

> And now, God, about the pink dress. You've seen me in that old white organdy for two years . . . and I'm grateful . . . I guess, but just this once, God, couldn't You open up Your treasure house and let me have a *pink* dress? . . . Tonight will most likely be the last chance I have to ask you for it, because the party is tomorrow night. You won't forget the time of the party is 7:30, will You, God? And please, ...*please* . . . send me the pink dress.

I walked over to the library table where the large family Bible rested between my mother's two tall silver candlesticks, and I tried to add on a last provision to my prayers, but it stuck in my throat. I couldn't yet say, "If it be thy will, let me have the pink dress." I wanted that dress any way I could get it.

I remember the moment when I knew that I was going to get the dress. I had walked away from the table and the Bible, and I heard the strains of "The Wedding March" from the church next door where prayer meeting was just ending. My parents had both gone to the service, but I asked permission not to go because, as I told my father, I had to stay home to struggle with the devil in case I didn't get the dress. He grinned, patted me on the head, told me to lock the screen door, and urged me to remember that he and my mother would be asking God for the pink dress too.

Soon I heard "The Wedding March" almost without realizing it. But a sensation of complete fulfillment came over me, and I knew that the pink dress was on the way. Shortly afterward, my parents came rushing up on the porch. I unlocked the screen door, and I saw their faces. My father was smiling broadly, and my mother, tears streaming down her face, was holding out her hand full of money! "Your pink dress, Betsy. You're going to get it!" My reply was, "Yes, I know."

Then they began pouring out the unbelievable story. Mrs. Askew had dashed into the church as the first hymn was ending. She seemed terrified, and gasped that she had just had a vision from her favorite medium, an Indian, who appeared often to her with advice of what to do. This time, it was a man instead of the usual woman medium, but the warning was clear: "Don't interfere any longer in your daughter's wedding or something dreadful will happen to you."

She had run from her home on the other side of the church, and she demanded that my father marry Amelia and Ben immediately. Ben and Amelia were both at prayer meeting—it was one of the few places where they could see each other—and they stood up right then and there, and my father married them before Mrs. Askew could recover from her fright and change her mind. Ben was so happy to get Amelia at last that he gave my father twenty-five dollars. My mother held out the money for me to see. "I'll get the *mousseline* tomorrow, and I'll make the dress in time for your party."

My father said, "You know that this is God's work, don't you? He had to change Mrs. Askew, and after all these years, that certainly couldn't have been easy."

Suddenly, we became aware that Chief Green Feather was standing in the doorway, and beaming proudly. He pointed to himself and said, "Now *I* am Great Spirit Messenger!" And it dawned on us that he had been the Indian medium that night who had appeared to Mrs. Askew. Overhearing our conversation about the dress, he had taken his way of getting it for me. But I knew how I really got the dress.

The next day, Jed asked me if I was still going with him to the party, and I assured him that I was. I told him I'd be ready at 7:00, all dressed up in the pink dress because God was sending it to me. Jed eyed me wonderingly and said, "You're the strangest girl I've ever known, but I like you—you're so different."

"Yes," I replied, "that's because I'm parsonage."

So I learned at twelve about personal prayer, and throughout all the years from then until eighty-five, I have been practicing my personal relationship with my Creator. I have gone through stages of praying, from the infantile "crisis" stage of "God, please get me out of this thing I've gotten myself into," to the more mature phase of sharing everything with God, especially the joy and gratitude I feel for life and its gifts. I've tried to bargain with God, and, sometimes the heavens were a brass wall against which "my voice echoed into nothingness." But I have never doubted that God was there, waiting for my call, and all I have to do is to make the connection. Without the experience of the pink dress, I might never have entered into a relationship that opened up all the resources I needed later on in life, when my own had been exhausted.

Adding on the provision that my father advised has not always been easy. To pray that something will happen "if it be thy will" means that whatever the result, it will be accepted. Such a blind leap of faith, which, as a parsonage child, was inherent in my growing up, requires that any prayer has to be under the condition that "if it be thy will." I'm learning to pray this kind of prayer with serenity because I am beginning, at eighty-five, to know that whatever is God's will can and will be right for me. If I can't have things the way I want them, then my prayer can help me to want the things that are best for me and to find a way to bring this about through my partnership with God.

I have had so many proofs that my prayers have been answered that I never question that. It's just that prayer is not always answered in my way. Then I know that I have not yet found the best way, and, together, God and I will continue the search. So, prayer is communion more than communication, and it is a two-way line.

5.
At Sixteen:
I Unlearn Prejudice

When I was twelve, my father joined the armed services as a chaplain in World War I and was sent back to North Carolina to Camp Greene at Charlotte. We packed all our worldly goods and left with mixed feelings—glad to be going back home, but sad to be leaving behind our adopted state, its friends and associations. We reached our temporary base in Charlotte where my mother and I were to be housed until my father was sent overseas. I entered high school in Charlotte, and for the first time in my life, I was in an all-white classroom. In all my elementary grades, there had been my Cherokee friends whose skin, although different from mine, had never made us different from each other in other ways, and I had grown accustomed to my classroom being people, not skin colors. But here, everyone was white, and I couldn't understand it for a while; but before too long, this seemed to be the "right" way.

I Learn About Death

Just as my father was expecting to receive orders to go overseas, the flu epidemic swept like a tide over the land, and soldiers in the camp were dying by the hundreds. My father was kept in Camp Greene to serve the vast number of soldiers needing his support and his comfort. So Mother and I remained in our apartment, and I continued in school.

The armistice was signed in November 1918, and my father left the Army and rejoined the Methodist Conference, meeting fortuitously in Charlotte just a week after the armistice. There was no problem about my father's transfer from the Eastern North Carolina Conference where he had been serving before we left for Oklahoma, nor the transfer to the Western North Carolina Conference from the Oklahoma Conference. In late November we went to serve a church not far from Charlotte, and I entered school there. The flu epidemic became worse, and everything was closed. No more than three persons were permitted to assemble at one time in one place, and all public meetings were forbidden. But here in this lovely little town with its one Methodist church we could talk in the open air and visit from one another's front porches. One of the teachers, who lived across the street from me, suggested to my parents that she teach me on her front porch each morning while the weather permitted, and, in this way, I might not lose the whole grade when the school reopened. My best friend joined me, and throughout the months of the epidemic, we went to Miss Horne for our schooling. It was a great experience, and we both progressed so well with her help that when school started again, we both took tests and went on to the next grade.

During the months when schools and churches were closed, the young people helped in every way they could. I rode all over the surrounding countryside with the town doctor and carried hot soup to those too sick to do anything for themselves. We didn't go inside the homes, but we delivered the jars of hot soup at the doors where someone would take them in. In many homes, there was no one able to come to the door to take the soup, and I would open the door slightly and set the jar down just inside the room. Death was everywhere, and funerals were commonplace. My father was on call day and night, and he and the doctor worked as a team.

I have a clear recollection of one morning when I walked next door from my home to the church and saw the front doors of the church open. I went slowly inside and down the aisle to the chancel rail where I saw a casket open. I walked up beside it and looked at the figure lying inside. It was my Sunday school teacher, a beautiful young woman who had caught the disease and had died so suddenly that the word had not gotten out. Her family wanted her body to rest in the church briefly. With all the doors open, and only one or two people coming in at a time, I suppose it had seemed safe enough.

My father came in and saw me standing there. He must have been concerned at my seeing death so starkly, without preparation— especially the death of my teacher whom I liked so much. He put his arm around my shoulder, hugged me, and suggested that we walk home together for lunch. On the way he talked to me in simple terms about what was happening and what death meant, but I do not recall that he scared me in any way—it all seemed a natural part of a plan, like leaves falling in the autumn and flowers springing up in early summer. I thank him for preparing me for this inevitable conclusion to life and for the relationship of death to its aftermath.

I was going to have to grow into my own conviction later on that death is life's most creative event. I had to develop a personal spiritual belief on my own. I am grateful that I do not, at eighty-five, have a "borrowed" faith. Because of my parents' encouragement of my individual search for identity, plus my parsonage upbringing that enveloped me in the assurance that this was a universe governed by a Creator who loved all of creation, I never thought of a God of vengeance and anger. God is my heavenly Father, whom I can trust.

I Unlearn Prejudice

By the time I was sixteen, we had moved twice more and were then living in a large city with one major high school. In November I went to school to register and be assigned to classes. I was intimidated by the size of the school, and, of course, as a stranger I faced the ordeal of having no acquaintances in my senior year. However, change was such a way of life for me that I took it in stride, I suppose. I do remember that I had butterflies when I was registered by a stern lady who glared at me over thin rimmed glasses. I had the feeling she wished that this new girl had not come in November to make new problems in keeping classes evenly balanced. I was assigned to an English class with Miss Stratton and to "Judge" Carl B. Hyatt for American History. Although I didn't know it at the time, fortune was again on my side.

In later years when I knew what I owed to these teachers, I wrote this tribute to Miss Stratton, first as a letter to the editor of the Winston-Salem, North Carolina *Journal,* and then following her death to North Carolina EDUCATION (Vol. XXVI, No. 9, p. 17, May 1960).

> . . . I came to understand rather suddenly and excitedly that this language of ours was a living force for communication of ideas and communion of feeling. And soon my adolescent imagination was being stirred by the magic of words, by the rhythm of spoken poetry, by analyses of human values inherent in the literary products of men's minds, by the architectural beauty apparent in the structure of sentences, paragraphs, compositions. Rules were "discovered" by us, and thus rarely disturbed us since we knew the "how" and the "why."
>
> She expected of each student a high degree of excellence, but, in retrospect, I now know that she recognized that there would be varying degrees of perfection. In her discernment, she capitalized on these differences, urging each one to appraise his/her own efforts, to be ever critical of results, to be ashamed to do less than his/her best. We were never compared with anyone else . . . only with our own past efforts. She had exacting requirements and great

expectations for each of us, and she led us to develop great expectations for ourselves.

She was my own best example to follow when, in 1926, I became an English teacher and learned a lot more from some of my students! But I am indeed grateful that my path led to her door that day in a new high school, and that under "her exacting, patient, and encouraging aegis, I was made aware of the need to 'get wisdom, but with wisdom, get understanding.' "

Between classes that first day, one of the other students walking beside me to my next class, said, "Judge Hyatt is a hard taskmaster, but he's a great teacher. You'll learn more than history from him." I asked why he was *Judge* Hyatt, and my companion explained that he had served as a judge, but that he was really a teacher who wanted to make history come alive for students who would become forces in that history, either negatively or positively. He'd seen the results of some of the negative attitudes in the court sessions, so he came into teaching.

We walked into the classroom, and I saw a broad-shouldered man at a desk in the front of the room. He was talking to some students, but when I entered the room, he came immediately to me, shook my hand, and welcomed me to the class. I wondered if he really was glad to see one more student to teach, one more name to add to the long roll, one more paper to grade; but I soon learned that I really was a welcome addition to his class, for I was one more student to introduce to a living history. For Judge Hyatt history walked, breathed, fought, and lived in that classroom, and because of him, I am a devotee of history as a story of people who made it.

It was he who taught me about prejudice—not by lecturing, but through one vivid experience. One day in the spring, about six weeks before the end of my senior year, Judge Hyatt started off the class by announcing that "*that* time has come." A groan with smiles went up all over the room, but I didn't know what it meant. His next words clarified it.

"Class, by tomorrow you should have selected the topic for your semester report. This is to be the paper you write to reveal your knowledge of the man or woman whom you choose as the greatest American. I'd like you to list three choices so that I can evaluate your basis for making value judgments. I'll leave it to you to choose the final name, but my interest at present is in the choices you make for the three persons whom you would list as great Americans. Important is not only *whom,* but *how* you came to select these people. Let me have your choices tomorrow in class, and the paper is due two weeks before graduation. The value of this paper is very high—it shows many things about you as you graduate, so it counts one-third of your final grade in this course." (This meant no one could graduate without it!) But this project fascinated me, and I began thinking about the people I considered great Americans. I asked my parents whom they would choose, and we had a lot of fun discussing our selections. But I had made up my mind that evening, and I wrote my names on a piece of paper with a feeling of smug superiority!

We turned in our lists to Judge Hyatt and went on with the class. I was already so sure of what I had done that I went to the library and checked out several books about my choice. The next day Judge Hyatt started the class by remarking that the class had shown remarkable acumen in their selections, and he handed back the lists with his approval. When he gave me mine, I looked down at it and read "See me after class!" I thought he was going to be especially congratulatory, and I wasn't worried.

I went up to his desk when the bell rang. He looked at me silently for a moment, and then he said, "Who were your three choices?" I told him I had written "Robert E. Lee, Robert E. Lee, Robert E. Lee." Three times the same name. He asked me why. I told him because Robert E. Lee was a great southern gentleman and leader in the Civil War. Judge Hyatt asked me if I had any other choices, and I said I didn't. Lee was my only choice. At that moment he looked straight into my eyes and he said, "You may not write about Robert E. Lee."

I couldn't believe I was hearing him. I just looked at him. He repeated, "You may not write about Robert E. Lee. Make another choice."

I was angry, so angry I stammered; but I told him I considered him undemocratic, that he was depriving me of my right of free choice, and that he had no right to take away that privilege, especially in a history class! How I dared to say these things, I'll never know, but my anger made me foolhardy and disrespectful to a man I admired so much. Maybe that was the reason—I never expected it from him. He said to me, "I have a responsibility to you as a student. You already know about Robert E. Lee, and apparently have made an idol of him. That is your privilege. My privilege as a teacher is to expand your horizons, to open new doors to you—and you need a new door opened! My decision is that you are to write your report about Abraham Lincoln."

I was stunned into silence and then exploded. Write about Abraham Lincoln, a northerner who had started the Civil War and had destroyed the South! How could he want me to know more about this man? Judge Hyatt heard me out and replied, "Because you need to know more about him. Your ignorance is appalling, and your prejudice is frightening. Write about Abraham Lincoln or flunk this course." I walked out in a daze, and my anger knew no bounds! He was unfair, and my parents would see that the principal knew about this.

When I reached home, my mother and father knew by my expression that something had happened. We called a family council at once, and I laid the case before them. When I finished telling them about Judge Hyatt's unfairness and his decision, I told them I wanted them to take the matter up with the principal. They said they would talk it over and after dinner we'd talk again. I knew my parents never had interfered by going to a principal, but this seemed an open and shut matter. I expected them to tell me that they would do something about it.

When we met after dinner, my father said in so many words that they were not going to go to the principal, but they were going to write a letter of appreciation to both Judge Hyatt and the principal for taking measures to dislodge me from my prejudices. He went on to point out that he and my mother had viewed my bigotries with growing alarm, and they had not been sure of how to deal with this. "You used to be able to search for facts about a subject, but lately you seem to be trying to prove, not what is right, but that you are right. Your strong biases bother us—especially your emotionalism when your 'rightness' seems at risk. So your mother and I are grateful to Judge Hyatt, and we consider it good fortune for all of us that he is your teacher."

I couldn't believe what I was hearing, but from my parents' decision there was no appeal, and with very poor grace, I accepted the situation. The next day I went to the city library and asked at the desk where to find some books about Abraham Lincoln. The librarian referred me to the shelves at the back of the long room, and there I was overcome at the great number of books about this man whom I had refused to consider "great." I went back to the desk and asked the librarian to suggest something I could begin with. I explained that this was for Judge Hyatt's class. She smiled and said, "I know." She listed three books for me. "Try the first one on the list; it will make a good introduction for your other reading." That book was one about Sara Bush Johnson, Lincoln's other mother, and I took it home, along with the two others of a more documentary nature.

Grudgingly, I took the books to my room after dinner and settled down to reading. I dreaded doing this, but I knew I had to start. To my surprise once I started on the book about Lincoln's other mother, I couldn't put the book down. The woman fascinated me—this woman who, as a stepmother, had taken over the family of Tom Lincoln and had encouraged the young boy, Abe, to dare his best efforts under the heaviest of obstacles and to believe in himself. I read on into the night until, at two o'clock in the morning, my mother came to check on me and saw the light under the door. She gently tapped on the door, told me how late it was, and said I should go to bed. I obeyed, but I was obsessed with the story and life of Sara Bush Johnson, and I began to "see through a glass darkly" the life of the boy and the man she had motivated to exert his strength against odds to reach the presidency.

I slept little that night. I was eager to get on with my reading and with writing the report. In the days that followed, I read voraciously. In fact, I swung so far over to the other extreme that my parents had to advise me to look for adverse points as well as positive ones to reach a fair picture of Lincoln. At that time of unlearning a prejudice, it was important not to go to the extreme of a prejudice *for* to the exclusion of facts that were negative. I was then at a critical crossroads: to differentiate between education and propaganda, something very important in all the years of my life, but especially at eighty-five.

I read and read and read, and finally the report was ready. I was proud of it. On the appointed day, I turned it in to Judge Hyatt, with two more weeks to go before graduation. I do not recall having thought much about the grade he would give me; I was thinking more about my own change of feeling about Lincoln. I now valued that "wonderful world of differences" and the interesting diversities that enriched our lives; I thought more about fairness, about the dangers of misinformation or lack of facts, about biases, about apathy. Judge Hyatt had taught me more than history; he had led me into pondering deep thoughts.

He returned the reports the next week. My paper had an "A" on it and a note that I cherished as long as the paper lasted. In red ink for emphasis, he had written and underlined, "Congratulations! This day you have become a student. Now, you can, if you wish, write about Robert E. Lee."

When all the students had left the room, I approached his desk. I said, "Judge Hyatt, I want to thank you, and my parents want to thank you. You have taught me a needed lesson, and it isn't in the history book. I know that I didn't need to know anything else about General Lee—I already knew about him and admired him. But Abraham Lincoln was a stranger to me, and my ignorance and bias kept him a stranger to me until you required me to learn about him. I am so glad that I was assigned to your class and that I have had you as my teacher of history. You are a great teacher, for you have taught me to be prejudiced!"

He was shocked at my final sentence. The look of consternation on his face showed me that he was upset. "How did I teach you to be prejudiced? That was what I was trying to correct in you."

He was deeply hurt, I'm sure, until I added: "You have taught me to be forever prejudiced against prejudice of any kind. This is something more valuable than a grade of "A," although I am very proud of such a grade from you. Thank you for everything—I shall never forget you." And I never have. At eighty-five, I'm still thanking him.

I Learn to Imagine

As I was learning from Judge Hyatt to seek all points of view before making a judgment, and from Miss Stratton the joy of self-expression, a past experience was "ringing a bell" with me—a *déjà vu*. For this was something that had happened also in another place, lingering until the present moment plugged it in. Back in the sixth grade, Miss Capshaw had made her students aware of "things that weren't there but could be if we made them be." She was the strictest teacher and one most feared in my school, but as a teacher in a new state, a "pioneer" herself, she sensed that her students must seize opportunities wherever they were, and wherever there didn't seem to be any opportunities, to create them and make them into realities. So, on Wednesday and Friday afternoons, we laid aside our books, and the classroom became our world as we made it. Her only rule was that the experiences should be those that we all would enjoy, and the results those in which we could take pride. Wonderful things happened in that classroom, and Wednesday and Friday afternoons became "red-letter occasions" for which we lived.

I remember vividly our "orchestra" in which we played imaginary instruments, taking care to play as if we were performing with the real thing: one girl fingering the cello, the boy playing drums and cymbal with abandonment, I playing the desk as a piano. We knew when we played a wrong note or went astray in rhythm. We felt keenly our responsibility to the entire orchestra, for, to us, it was real. As we revelled in the rewards of creation, we added gradually the drama of making plays out of stories we read, of having characters from a folk tale speak the authentic words we put in their mouths, and of reading, reading, reading, and writing, writing, writing! The language arts really came alive in Miss Capshaw's room—we read and listened in order to learn from others; we spoke and wrote to express ideas of others and of ourselves.

Here was a teacher who was firm, strict, and even sometimes rigidly demanding; yet she led us so joyously and excitedly with a sense of true adventure into a world where things were not always as they ought to be, but where things could be as they ought. She taught us that we could evoke changes if we brought them into being, if we ventured to try ideas not yet tried, if we explored logically and courageously, if we sensed imaginatively, and if we had a sense of pride in our accomplishments. She opened doors of creative expression to us, and we found a new and exciting world beyond.

Teachers played a very important role in my life, and perhaps it is because of what many of them did for me that I determined to be a teacher. The earliest moment that I recall voicing that goal was when I was eight years old, and someone asked me that familiar question so often asked of children and youth, "What do you want to be when you grow up?" I seemed to be very certain, even at that early age, and I never swerved from that purpose, although my reasons probably became more rational. I answered that I wanted to be a teacher. My reason at eight was, "As a teacher, I can write on the blackboard whenever I want to."

Once, when I told my father that if I had been a boy, I would probably have become a minister as he was, he said something I never forgot. "If you do hold to this early decision to be a teacher, remember this: I, as a minister, can only affect the lives of those who choose to attend my church and stay awake to listen to what I have to say. My influence upon them is limited. But as a teacher of all the children of all the people in the public school, you will touch the lives of the world in a way I'll never be able to do. Use your position or power in your classroom to meet them where they are, and lead them where they can become whatever they can become in their own way. Never exploit them—their good is your good. Let them make you a real teacher!"

In my teaching and in professional relationships with others in the years ahead, I sensed how important it is that those over whom I had any kind of power should never be exploited for any cause, never used, never cheated of their own dignity through the use of sarcasm or ridicule. To humiliate someone intentionally meant not only harm to that person, but such action reduced me to a low level as well.

Through the years of teaching teenagers and young adults, I became especially alert to my own ethical relationships with those over whom I held power. I realized the destructiveness of methods of control that undermined the self-esteem and dignity of my students. I'm sure that my actions in the classroom and with my professional peers was human enough to bring about negative reactions at times, but when I realized that I was being unfair, I stopped and tried to rectify the situation. My perceptions became keener in my relationships with others. I even became more aware of my humor and how its honest laughter might hurt sensitive youth.

Learning to be eighty-five makes me remember that I learned to be sixteen when one teacher taught me the beauty and the disciplined order of my mother tongue, and another released me from the bondage of prejudice. I graduated and went on to college, realizing there how much I owed these teachers. Today, at eighty-five, the debt mounts even higher, to be repaid only as I translate into relationships with my world the timeless teachings of those who inspired me.

I have often wondered about what I actually taught those hundreds of boys and girls who sat in my classroom through what were perhaps the most important years of their lives. I have wondered what a grade of A, B, C, or F did for them and to them, and what the lasting effects of our times together meant. Whatever these effects were, they started in the classroom and went out from there, in ever widening circles, into the world that was theirs—theirs to inherit and theirs to make. If an excitement for learning began in my class, if wonder initiated an eternal quest for new adventures in gaining knowledge and wisdom, then I did for them what my teachers did for me. I wish I knew!

6.
At Twenty-Four:
I Inherit Responsibility

My years from twenty to forty-five include many "teachable events," most of them filled with tumultuous change. Change should have been so natural for me that it just "happened," but the things I am about to describe happened so suddenly, with one following another in quick succession, that I couldn't adjust to one before another shattering variance dealt me a blow "below the belt." What was ahead for me would shake me loose from the moorings that had held me at safe anchor throughout my life.

Graduation from college in 1926 launched me into what the commencement speaker assured us was a world "waiting just for us." I was successful in getting my first job and took the position offered me in the town where my father was enlarging the church. I lived at home because my absence at college for four years made me want to re-establish my family ties, somewhat different since I was "on my own," but still ties that bound me to those who meant the most to me. I was enjoying my newfound financial independence with a munificent salary of eighty dollars per month for a school year of eight months. This was a fortune that I budgeted with tender loving care. I liked my work, although I soon discovered that the students did not behave as my college texts seemed to think they would. It took Gabe Weston to make me know what discipline meant. You either have the ability to maintain control and discipline or you don't. Finding out is a test of stamina and fortitude.

I Learn to Stand My Ground

Gabe didn't know that he was teaching me anything, and neither did I at the moment. I taught classes all day and supervised an assigned study hall during the last period where 125 squirming, tired teenagers were supposed to be studying in a large auditorium. The situation was not conducive either to study or to effective supervision, for the seats had no desk arms, the lighting was dim, and I couldn't keep up with everyone after I checked the roll at the start of the period! Students would be in their seats for the first five minutes, and then some would drop to the floor beneath the seats and crawl all over the auditorium where I could not see them. The noise was distracting, and even those who wanted to study, couldn't.

For me, it was an ordeal I didn't intend to let go on, but I didn't know how to correct it. I did know that the uneasiness with which I faced this last period of the day was destroying the joy I felt in teaching my regular classes. I have often wondered why a principal would expose a beginning teacher to such a "trial by fire" in her first teaching experience, but, in retrospect, I suppose it is better to find out who can come through such a test and be able to control a classroom before one becomes a fixture and has a class associate disorder with learning. I faced this last period with genuine dread, and each day I felt less like a teacher and more like a police officer. Study hall was turning me against my chosen profession, and I might not have stayed if it hadn't been for Gabe.

He was a football player, and a good one. Thus, Gabe had a special place of hero worship in the student body. Furthermore, his father was on the school board and controlled my job. I had tried to stay in with Gabe, but in doing so, I had apparently lost his respect. One day, just after I had checked the roll and found his seat vacant, he came clumping down the aisle in his football shoes, headed for the side door of the auditorium that opened out upon the football field—another hazard to a manageable study hall! I watched him march down to the aisle that led to the door, and I realized that the gauntlet had been thrown down. Gabe was going to prove that he could do whatever he wanted to in this study hall, and he intended to go out to football practice instead of staying in his assigned place.

I met him face to face as he was turning into the side aisle. The battle was joined, and the study hall was still with tension. He was grinning at me and kept coming. I crossed my arms and stood as firm as my trembling legs would let me. Bracing my body against the seat behind me, I asked him where he was going. He humored me with a condescending smile and said he was reporting to football practice. I looked him in the eyes and, controlling my breath as best I could, I told him that he was due to be in this study hall and he was to take his seat. He had stopped in the middle of the center aisle, and I faced him, scared to death, but angry at his disrespect. I knew that if I lost this contest, I would lose control of any class, for the word would go out far and wide from that group of students that Gabe had "bested" the teacher, and I would be fair game from then on.

I asked him again to sit down, and he asked me what I would do if he didn't. I told him he would have to move me out of his way to get out the door and he'd do that over my dead body. We were locked in grim eye-to-eye combat, and he started to put his arms out to lift me by my elbows. He could have done it easily, for he was a giant as he stood over me. I doubt if I could have moved if I had wanted to, but after locking his gaze into mine, his arms dropped slowly and, most importantly, his eyes sought the floor. I sensed that I had won; the one who can outstare the other proves stamina at least, if not good sense. He later told some other students that he was all set to lift me out of his way, but my face was white and my eyes were steel-gray and glinting with anger, and he knew better than to touch me. He turned and took his seat, and my days of trouble with student behavior belonged to the past. Gabe taught me not so much how to control students, but, rather, how to control myself, and this important lesson was to save my life later in my teaching experience.

I Lose My Father

At the end of that first year of teaching, a particularly advantageous position opened up for me in a school system near the new church to which my parents had been moved. For the next six years I learned as much or more than I taught. It was during that period of my life, in 1929, that my father died suddenly from pneumonia. Penicillin, discovered in London in 1928, was not in wide use at that time, and other antibiotics and treatments were not available. Within two days, he was gone.

My mother and I had gone home late in the afternoon to get some rest, but we were summoned back to the hospital at two o'clock in the morning. It was one of the worst nights, weatherwise, that the area had experienced, and I called a friend to drive us to the hospital. I still remember that although numb from the approaching loss of my father, I sensed the perilous nature of that drive over streets iced into glassiness—much of the way uphill. We made it, but I consider it a miracle of driving skill and prayer, for no cars were moving that night, not even taxis.

The hospital was quiet, and only my father's labored breathing broke the silence in his room. We kept a vigil through that night, and as his hand ceased to respond to my clasp, I knew that I was suddenly and without preparation, the responsible head of our family. This idea was frightening, and my grief at losing my father doubled the shock.

This change was too sudden, too traumatic for me to accept as a habitual circumstance, and I learned to be twenty-four within a moment's time—when my father's hand loosened his grip on mine. My mother and I now were our family, and life went on but in a different way. My job was our only financial support, although my father left a small insurance policy, all that his salary through the years allowed. With the help of a lawyer friend of my father's, I settled the estate and, when the insurance was paid, I placed the money in the local bank as a nest egg for my mother.

I Become Head of the Household

In 1929 and into the 1930's the Great Depression created trauma for millions. With my mother depending upon me and with my job being all that we had between us and a void of uncertainty, I found that my ability to pray and to have faith grew in proportion to my need for guidance. Getting that pink dress years before had created the lines of communication between me and my Creator, but this situation was making demands from my own abilities. I did all that I could do, and then I simply laid my situation in God's hands. I do not know nor can I explain how things worked out, but they always did, although my own power was tested to the limit. I discovered within myself ways of finding solutions that I had never known were there, and I found that people with solutions were there when they were needed. I was so persistent in prayer that, later, I often thought that God must have been so busy taking care of me that other people had to wait. At any rate, the stress was great, and I paid for it with my own health. I never broke down, but tension became a daily companion.

Then change again made a mighty difference. In 1933, most of the local banks failed, and the one in which I had deposited the insurance money closed for good (or bad, in my case). I never received a penny of that money afterward. On March 6, 1933, President Franklin D. Roosevelt declared a bank holiday and closed all banks in the United States to help stop a money panic. Depositors had been withdrawing their money so fast that banks ran out of money to pay people over the counter. I recall seeing trucks pull up to one large "chain" bank, and it never reopened. All the school money for financing the school system of the area was in that bank, and for the next year, our school system was taken over by the state legislature to supervise its management and to pay the teachers in scrip.

The pay check I had deposited just before the bank closing was frozen, and, of course, ceased to be available to me. The insurance money was gone, and I had ten cents left in my pocket that day. I was on my way to the bank to cash a check when I got the word that the bank would not open for business. My mother had fifteen cents, and we had about half a tank of gas in my father's car that I had inherited and learned to drive (in a rather horrendous way). I went immediately to the bank where crowds of depositors were gathered, some crying, others beating on the door, still others numb with shock, too dazed to do more than just look around for answers to unspoken questions. I got to the door and read the notice. No money now, and no predictable date when there would be any.

During that day some of the leading citizens and officials in the community ended their own lives; and the papers reported, both in print and in picture, the shock waves of grief and anguish spreading out to the far sections of our community. I remember that an acquaintance of mine, a teller in the bank that failed with my money, told me some time later how much she wanted to warn me not to deposit my check, for she knew that the bank would be closed. But legally she could not advise me and she said, "If you can, remember that I turned away when you came to my window to fill out your deposit slip. I could not do this for you without crying—I knew what was going to happen to you, and I could not prevent it nor tell you about it!"

These were very dark days for that entire community, but we seemed to draw together in a new way and to form a partnership among ourselves in the effort to help one another survive. Parents of the children I taught shared their farm products with us, and, somehow, we managed. I had a small life insurance policy on which I found I could borrow for the little cash I needed to supplement the scrip salary my job was bringing in. Miracles happened and things went on. Teachers taught, children learned (a lot of it not in books), parents helped, merchants cooperated, and a new spirit was born in that community. In reality, we became neighborhoods of friends seeking ways to help one another.

But change wasn't through with me and others around me. My mother's health, which had not been good since my father's death, appeared to be deteriorating. One morning, when I got up to get ready to go to school, I found her lying in bed, looking up at the ceiling without moving. I could get a response from her hand, but she could not speak or move her body. I called for help from our doctor friend who lived across the street, and he was there in moments. She had had a stroke and would need constant care. I had to be at school, and the doctor said he would send a member of his family over until I had time to make some plans. I was in a daze, but as soon as help arrived, I went on to school, for my job was all that we had except for the most frantic praying I had ever done.

Word about my mother had spread quickly, and the students offered me their heartfelt sympathy, most of it unspoken, for they did not quite know what to say nor how to say it. But I knew what they were trying to do, and it was a wonderful day to remember—their understanding gave me a conviction that youth have a great capacity for unselfish caring, and this came through to me that day. Even the boy who was a troublemaker at times smiled at me as he deliberately threw a spit ball at the blackboard and said, "I thought I'd liven things up a little—just to be normal." We laughed, and it helped.

When the money was gone and there was none in sight, Ruby showed up at my kitchen door one morning and said, "I heard you needed someone to stay with your mother and take care of her during the day. I've come to help." I didn't know who she was, but she had a note from the mother of one of my students telling me what a wonderful person Ruby was and ending with, "She needs you now as much as you need her. Help each other." I told Ruby that I couldn't pay her anything, and she said all she needed was three meals a day and she'd cook them. I told her I couldn't accept this for nothing, and she only replied, "I've been used to helping someone for a long time, and he's not here to help any longer. I don't want to get out of practice." That was all that we ever said about this, and Ruby was an answer to prayer. She stayed on with us until my mother was strong enough to do her usual household chores. And that was another miracle.

One morning as I was leaving for school, the telephone rang. It was my uncle from another state calling to tell us that my mother's only sister and my beloved aunt had died unexpectedly the night before. The funeral would be in two days at the old home place in eastern North Carolina. Would Mother be able to come? I was just saying that she couldn't because of the stroke, when to my amazement, I heard my mother say, "Yes, I will be there!" I turned around and she was sitting up in bed and speaking for the first time since the stroke. She and I were equally stunned and simply looked at each other for a minute before I told my uncle that Mother was moving and speaking, and if the doctor approved, we would come down for the funeral. We did, and my mother regained her mobility and speech. She seemed to be without any apparent serious aftereffects from the stroke. (I realized later that she was weakened on one side.) When I asked the doctor how she had so suddenly moved and spoken, he said that in all likelihood the shock of hearing me talking to my uncle about my aunt's death had been a countershock that brought back her movement. I never understood how it happened—I just knew that something happy had changed our lives again. Ruby rejoiced with us and stayed until my mother was able to become active again—which she insisted on doing as soon as she could. When Ruby left us, it was like letting a family member go. She often visited us, and we learned that her being with us had enabled her to come out of a period of great bereavement herself. When she left that last day, she said something to us that I have always cherished. Embracing the two of us, she remarked, "I love you because you're so common—just like me!" A great compliment from a truly great lady.

Another change that had seemed like a disaster—and it was, temporarily—proved to be a great benefit to me. In a way it reminds me of that day when my father was thrown from the motorcycle into Dallas Eicherhorn's Laughing Mule Saloon. It seemed like a catastrophe, but my father turned it into his—and Dallas's—advantage just by the way he used Dallas's dare when we were newcomers to town. I didn't consciously do anything but things worked out to my advantage through something I had done and forgotten about. When the Depression came, and when the people stood in line for food, for places to sleep, for tissues, for bobby pins, and for stockings to wear in the cold, I was assured of my job at least, with its monthly scrip payment that the local merchants honored. I had been in that school system for six years, and had managed to earn my master's degree—don't ask me how; it was just another miracle. But the Depression had caused such scarcity of funds everywhere that our school system had, like others, decided to streamline the teaching staffs and let those who were not local people return to their own communities. It was a fairly widespread feeling that in these hard times, each community needed to take care of its own, so I wasn't worried about having a job. But my teaching certificate had been issued as a "blanket certificate" that allowed me to teach out of my field for a proportionate part of my teaching load. There had never been a problem with this before, but now my principal informed me that, since he was letting a teacher go, I would need to assume part of her teaching load. I would have to teach a subject in which I knew I was not competent. I knew that this would be unfair to the students who shared my ignorance and that I would have been a total wreck within a week. So, after talking things over with my mother, who agreed with my decision, I informed the principal that I could not remain under those circumstances; and I stepped out in faith into joblessness.

I began looking for a position, and to help us through the summer, I worked as a filing clerk for a government agency. I knew that this would destroy my sanity in a few weeks because all I did all day long was alphabetize names and file them. I missed teaching boys and girls, and I kept on searching for a way to get back into the classroom. One day someone called to tell me about an opening in a county not too far from where I lived. I went for an interview, and the first question asked me was "What political party do you belong to?" I left, refusing the position that was later offered me. As I drove back home on an almost empty tank of gas, I was really frightened at my jobless state. I felt I had nowhere to turn. I found out on that ride back that work is essential to a person's identity in a society that is work-oriented, and it is requisite to a person's achievement and self-respect. I needed a job—work I was trained to do. Feeling very much alone, I prayed all the way home, desperately wanting someone to help me.

When I walked in the door later that afternoon, my mother informed me that I had had a telephone call, and she gave me a number to call. It was the number of the large city school system where I had graduated under the tutelage of Judge Hyatt and Miss Stratton, among others. The office of administration was calling to ask me to come for an interview at my earliest convenience! I was stunned.

When I phoned the person who had left the message, I asked him how he knew to call me. He said he was looking for a teacher with majors in my two fields and that he had found in the files an application of mine from several years back. I had forgotten all about applying there and certainly had not thought of looking for a job there with the present cutting back of staff. But they, too, were letting go all persons who were not local, and were looking for competent teachers in the area whom they could fit into the school system. This was too much for me to take in all at once, but I stammered out that I would come in the next morning for the interview.

I was offered the position of teaching exactly what I wanted to teach, and my extra duties were to direct glee club and whatever drama activities I wanted to try with the students. Change had indeed brought the positive back into my life, where lately it had seemed that I was accentuating the negative. ✓

Change had played havoc with my ordinary existence, and it had made me face choices that, at times, seemed only adverse. But along this road on which I was traveling to be eighty-five, such changes were necessary for me to grow into my later years. At one point I was told I had a fifty-fifty chance of having cancer. However, I had a physician who helped me win the battle by reminding me as I lay on the operating table awaiting lengthy and dangerous surgery, "I'm counting on you to fight with me through this. I'll do my best, but I can't do it by myself. You stay in there, and help me!" I remember looking up at him as I gave him my promise not to "drop out"; I didn't, and he didn't, and the two of us made it through.

A few years later, four eye operations raised my anxiety to fever pitch, but, again, the results were favorable. In recent years, a small percentage hearing loss has cost me some of my prized hearing ability, but my prior teaching experiences and training in speech and in music have afforded me understandings both of what is happening and how to compensate for this. Besides, when my face beside my mother's in the mirror at age seven helped me to find my identity and to accept myself as I was, whatever happened to me from then on got itself glued into the me I became in that event. This is extremely important as I learn to be eighty-five, for age sometimes distorts a self-image into something it is not, and then trouble results because there isn't a real "me" to deal with the real happening.

Illness was not the only thing that threatened my future. One day I faced death in my classroom. A disturbed girl, angry for no known reason, started creeping up on me as I stood at the blackboard explaining something. My back was turned, but I suppose the strange silence in the room alerted me. I turned to look over my shoulder, and the girl was almost upon me, eyes glaring with hate, and her hand was holding a knife raised to plunge into my back. Had I not turned, she would undoubtedly have killed me. Two boys in the class were sneaking up behind her to grab her, but they would have been too late. I managed not to frighten her by screaming or by trying to grab her; I made no attempt at any sudden move—in fact, I doubt if I could have, for her hand was beginning to descend with the knife. In some unexplainable way, Gabe came to my mind—don't take my eyes from an adversary. I fixed my eyes on hers and began to hum very softly in almost a monotone one of the glee club melodies. I could hardly get breath enough to hum, but I kept on holding her with my eyes. She stopped moving. Her hand froze about eight inches from my shoulder, and the glare began to fade from her eyes. After what seemed an eternity, her hand, still holding the knife, lowered, but not as a threat. I held out my hand to her, very slowly so as not to frighten her again, and she put the knife in my hand, slumping as if drained of all energy. I motioned to one of the boys to leave quietly and get the principal, and the other to help her back to her seat. Then, trying to act as if nothing untoward had happened, I went on with the class. I was very proud of that class, for those young people did everything right, and a real tragedy never happened.

The girl's parents were summoned to the school, and medical attention was sought for the girl. She did not return to this school, but she sent a note sometime later that said, "I'm sorry I tried to hurt you. It wasn't you I hated—you were just there." Today we would understand that the girl might well have been an abused child trying to get even with someone out of reach or unable to be faced. I grew up fast that afternoon, and Gabe helped me to stay alive.

These years brought valuable positives to offset the negatives. Change had turned strangers into friends and neighbors, and barriers had been broken. These were times of joy as well as of deprivation and loss, for a resilience in bouncing back from a liability turned troubles into assets created through resourcefulness. Where, before, we tended to buy what we didn't have, we learned to make what we needed, and our talents were encouraged by our need. We found something where something was not, and it was good. We were indeed accentuating the positive.

I Learn to Teach Self-Expression

Because of the need to be resourceful, the after-school activities of drama, speech, and creative writing became a school-accredited elective with an ever-growing number of students. The creative writing and subsequent play productions led to student participation and high interest that a teacher dreams about; these were students with unexplored creative abilities not demanded in traditional courses. Here, in original creations they could respond to individual ways of expression. Fascinating things happened, and every class was a revelation to them of what they could do. Their joy in learning was the main incentive, and our work began to assume almost a professional character. Certainly the attitude of the students did, for they were serious about their work and held themselves to high standards of performance. Many original plays were good enough to be entered in the state drama festival each year, and it was unusual if the students did not bring home at least one state award for playwriting and play production. From these creative classes there went out some whose plays were published and some who went to Hollywood to become actors. One person became a director. But, most importantly, those who enjoyed being creators just for personal enjoyment—and these were the majority—became appreciative of the arts and became a future public who would stimulate and encourage such appreciation in their communities.

Within the first year of this emphasis upon creative work, a club was formed named The Scribblers. Its members were those who, wanting to go beyond the limits of a fifty-minute class in school, decided to write for the fun of it. To remain in this organization, a person had to earn points voted on by the membership. For me to belong and remain in, I too, had to write. And write I did, relying upon many of the "learning events" out of my past to make into dramatic possibilities. The students were a continuing stimulus for my creating, and their writings were quite diverse. Some students I remember well, for they were unusual in so many ways, and quite individual in nature and reaction.

I remember Ray. We were studying poetry with a view to appreciating it as one way of understanding the person who wrote it. One poem that I enjoyed aroused Ray's raucous laughter as we read the first lines: "A garden is a lovesome thing, God wot!" Ray proclaimed it the silliest thing he'd every heard, and only some nut could ever think of such a thing, much less write about it in words like *lovesome*. "And what in the world does *God wot* mean?" he wanted to know. These words not only held no meaning for him—they turned him off.

As one who enjoyed poetry and who had accepted the definition that prose is the language of communication while poetry is the language of communion, I had to recognize that I could not fairly expect students to share my enthusiasm. I eyed Ray as objectively as I could, and I saw a big, husky, high school athlete to whom the word *lovesome* would, of course, be silly, and to whom *God wot* would be a foreign language. Many of the other students were nodding their heads in agreement.

I asked him what *he* would say if he were writing this poem, and he bluntly said, "I wouldn't write it at all." There was some applause from others in the room. I felt this was almost a personal insult, for the poet had put his thoughts and feelings into the way he wanted me to hear, but at that moment I also saw and heard it as Ray was hearing it—and he wasn't hearing the poet at all. I suggested that there might be something he wanted to say that used a poetic form, but he shrugged negatively. I urged him to give it a try and to let me see it the next day. I asked the class members to respond in their way to feelings they had about anything and to see if poetry allowed them to express their thoughts any differently than a prose statement did. They became interested in this, and the class ended on a positive note.

The next day Ray dropped a piece of paper on my desk, saying on "Well, here it is, and I did it my way." That he did the assignment at all encouraged me. I read the four lines that he had written his way, and it really was Ray as a poet! Here it is as he wrote it almost fifty years ago.

> He watched beside his hidden still.
> "Dag Nab, you keep away," he cussed.
> A shot rang out across the hill—
> A revenoor bit the dust!

I suppose that, out of respect for me, his "dag nab" was substituted for stronger language, but at least it did preserve the rhythm of the line.

And then I remember Jerry who, like many of our high school boys, later went out of the classroom to don a uniform in service to our country. Jerry wrote the following lines that would turn out to be an omen of his future:

> The shadows crept across the sky,
> The pilots talked, their planes near by;
> Things that to us make little sense
> Of the cow back home that jumped over the fence.
> They talked and talked, but little knew
> Who would come back, a lot or a few?
> "Back home," they start—they always do—
> Of the girl they love, and people they knew;
> Of Mom and Pop and Sister, too,
> and all the things they meant to do . . .
> But now as the hour draws dangerously near,
> And the "Bomber's Moon" overhead is clear,
> They jog to their planes with a silent gait

And think of some tricks they will use for bait . . .
They feel a deep pride as inward they slip,
And look and admire their own speedy ship . . .
There's no time now to talk or to play
All that must wait for another day.
They pull back the throttle, and off they fly
Down the runway and into the sky;
The guns on the wings seem only a toy,
But they knew they were there to kill and destroy.
A prayer on their lips as they go to attack,
"Please, dear God, please let me come back!"
They prayed and hoped, but little knew,
Who would come back, a lot or a few?

I remember Eleanor who came into our writing group when her
parents left Indonesia to escape the Japanese. The fascinating stories
she had to tell as she shared another culture with all of us were an
education in themselves, and her adjustment to our school and
community was made a little easier by her writing. She had a way with
words, and, although she was not talkative with others, her writing
revealed a brilliant mind and a disciplined manner of expressing ideas.
One poem she wrote I have kept through these years in a collection of
student writings. Eleanor called this poem "Moonlight Minuet," and I
often wondered what lay behind the words.

The moonlight and the shadows danced,
And I lay there and gazed, entranced.
'Twas such a strange and eerie sight—
These ghostly dancers in the night.

They bowed and curtsied in the hall
Or fluttered down the hard, cold wall.
The moonlight fop and shade coquette
Sedately danced the minuet.

They lightly swayed and whirled around,
And never did they make a sound.
They slid through cracks upon the floor,
And melted through the oaken door.

They danced o'er spider webs with grace,
Transforming gray to silver lace.
The shadows rustled silken skirts;

The moonbeams boasted ruffled shirts.

They tripped and glided through the room
And disappeared into the gloom.
The moonbeams fled at dawn of day—
The flitting shadows danced away.

And then there was Anna. I tried never to show favoritism to students, but Anna was memorable in a special kind of way. She had so far to go, and she went beyond any expectations. She was sent to the creative writing experience with the hope that this class might bring a new realization to her of who she was and what her great possibilities were. The class was a magnet drawing from her an ability she had never known she possessed; certainly she was a surprise to those who had tried to teach her and found her unresponsive. Her apparent isolation from social relationships made her a loner, aggressively searching on her own for an identity—and she was searching in her own way, which was sometimes disturbing to others.

In this class, however, where everyone was fired up with ideas and the exciting results, she began to express herself in surprising ways. One day she electrified us all with a metaphorical remark about a barren tree outside the window. Not rapidly, but progressively, she began to contribute to the class; the others enjoyed what she did and let her know it. By early spring she had written a one-act play, humorous yet poignant in its hidden meanings. The class voted to have it as their spring production. The audience applauded it wildly, and we entered the play in the state drama festival. It won for playwriting, and we then entered it in production. I shall never forget the night of the awards. It is not easy to win in that contest, but Anna's play won the best of the festival. When her name was called to come to the stage to receive the top award, she just sat in stunned disbelief. One of the students pulled her to her feet, and she stood, tears streaming down her face, as the audience began to shout, "Author! Author!" I saw Anna come into her own that night, and from then on there was no stopping her. She had wings, and could now fly on her own. Look at something Anna turned in as one of her first assignments; then read her post-award effort.

The Unimportant Things

Had I but one day left
To do the things I'd fill a lifetime with,

To think and say the things that must live on;
If all the years I've planned to fill with work and play
And just the joy of life were gone,
To gather all the beauty life affords
And know that all that matters most was done—
Had I one day to put it all into,
What would I do from rise to set of sun?

First, I think I'd get up early
To eat breakfast with my family.
I'd like to have my father
Put down his newspaper and really see me—
See me as I really am . . .
Not as the mirror shows me . . .

I think I'd leave my math book home
So I could borrow someone else's
And read the notes they so unwisely
Leave between the pages.
No one has ever written me a note like that . . .
But on this last day, it would be nice to get
Someone else's and pretend that it was meant
For me . . .

There was a great deal more to this poem. She had written, further in the piece, about me as her teacher—three things about me that she didn't like. Her ideas were perceptive and honestly expressed, and I acted on two of them at once. The third attribute I did not change. I felt it was important to trust students by putting them on their own, and she thought that I shouldn't do this because "trusting people before they're ready for it makes them easy targets for temptation." I saw a girl within a girl who, unrecognized for most of her life, now was breaking out and letting her world know that she was there. After the award for her excellent drama, she wrote the following lines:

Child's Paintbox

I like color!
The yellow of ungilded daffodils
That cheapens glittering gold. The purple of
The violets, Dogwood's rust and white;
The purest dewy white of lilies' sheen.

The pink and baby blue of hyacinths.

I like color!
The black of rich woods—dirt. The bronze of trees
In autumn, and the blue of autumn's sky.
The brown dust along a country road.
The frosty blue of asters, late and wild.
The heavy gray of smoke from campfire's warmth.

I like color!
The rose of sunrise and the silver-white
Of summer clouds. The gray of stealing dust,
The cardinal's red and jaybird's blue.
The purple, black, or scarlet of wild berries
On the hill. Straw-colored, new-mown hay.

I like color!
The red and white of berries on the snow;
The thin black smoke from houses huddled down;
The brown of cones and green of stately pines;
The holly's green and silver-blue of ice . . .
A rainbow made by icicle and sun . . .

O . . . I LIKE COLOR!

She no longer was so imprisoned within herself that she could not see the world outside. She could see it, enjoy it, revel in it—and tell about it.

So, in learning to be twenty-four to forty, I learned to lose all my financial security; to lose a job and gain a better one; to face fear and potential death in a classroom and in an operating room; to accept the realities of possible cancer and blindness; and to mature in my religious faith and to trust in God, others, and myself. I also learned to be grateful for life and its gift of aging. Especially in these years I learned from my young students how exciting learning can and must be. These young creators brought a spontaneity, a courage, an enthusiasm, a zest for searching, and a wonder about life and about their part in it that was a continuing inspiration for me to emulate. Later, I learned to spread my wings with theirs in seeking new possibilities and new eventualities.

7.
Becoming Older:
I Learn to Teach and Am Taught

Subconsciously I had sensed, as a teacher, the need to involve my adolescent students in seeking and finding their identities within the larger identity of their world. I wanted to help them see themselves as individuals but still feel ties to their heritage. They could draw from the world for their own enrichment, and they could feel a sense of importance by making individual contributions. Adolescents inhabit two worlds—theirs (which is all too often a lonely place), and the world as the way they wish it to be. If these two worlds do not touch significantly, adolescents must then create a world of their own—with their peers or without them—a world that satisfies them. In response I turned to discovering innovative forms of drama, especially of writing for theater.

In the pre-Hitler days in Europe, I had visited Oberammergau and had seen the last production of *The Passion Play* before its discontinuation. That production was an enthralling experience, but what took hold of my imagination and kept me attentive during the eight-hour performance was the grandeur of the magnificent speech chorus of fifty voices and golden-robed figures forming a living curtain between the audience and the actors. Their universal voice, speaking universal sentiments made me become a part of the action on the stage. I left that performance with a compelling need to know more about this form of drama, and how to use it with integrity with adolescents, for it would be easy to exploit them to achieve an effect rather than to direct them toward identity. The search would lead me into a new perceptiveness of who I was.

On one of my rare excursions to New York during a Christmas vacation, I succeeded in getting a ticket to a new play on Broadway, *Member of the Wedding,* starring Ethel Waters and a young Julie Harris. In the play, a young girl wanted desperately to be a part of a coming wedding, to feel related to this family event. Her longing was heart-rending to watch. I shall never forget that moment when, not yet knowing whether she would be included, she walked up to the curtain line, and with a premonition of failure, held up both arms in supplication and exclaimed, "All people belong to a 'we' except me." I remember how a stillness came over that audience as her prayer became a silent utterance that is shared universally.

When the curtain fell, the memory of that teenager, yearning to be "someone" with other someones, lingered in a breathless theater. Then the thunderous applause came and the lights came up, reflecting tears streaming down the faces of those who felt exactly as she did. This memory remained with me, and when I returned to my classroom after the vacation, that teenager was there in the face of every student before me. I saw young people who were trying to be a "me" without being absorbed in a "we."

My Oberammergau experience seemed to blend in with the pleas of the young girl in the Broadway play, and the two caused me to become more interested in and more knowledgeable about experimenting with this form of theater. I did not want just to produce something spectacular that would temporarily gratify the egos of students and teacher; I wasn't out to create an effect, but, rather, to see that any effect created was a natural result of a genuine educational experience.

With the students as co-searchers, we went to work. We needed a discipline based in serious study, so I went to the Northwestern University School of Speech where a special course in choric speaking was being offered that summer. Under the tutelage of a teacher who was a graduate of the University of London Speech Choir, I learned about this ancient art form as a way of universal expression, and I began to feel my way through the use of it with the adolescent drama class. During the next four years, as the speech choir proved itself with the students, I saw it as a stimulating procedure for an historical and experimental thesis for my doctoral dissertation. The students joined me in finding out whether my assumptions were valid and reliable. I developed a teaching technique for improving speech through choric speaking, and the final results more than justified my assumptions.

The students developed a "social sense," a feeling of belonging to something worthy. Many who had never dared to speak publicly alone, now felt quite comfortable in the group speaking, and some were even feeling a sense of value for their contributions as members of society. Also, because we were speaking poetry and rhythmical verse, their appreciation of literature was deepening. They were proud of what they did and ashamed if they fell short of their best expectations.

The principal sent Bill to the drama-speech-writing class in hopes that his participation would be a redemptive, healing process.

Bill was a born troublemaker and didn't know the meaning of the word *cooperation*. At first, he simply sat in the group, not participating. One day, however, he spoke out, and the class applauded his performance. From then on, Bill had "his lines," and he spoke them well.

One evening there was to be a public performance at the city auditorium, but Bill was denied the right to appear with the choir because of some rule infraction, so his lines were given to someone else. On the night of the public appearance, we were in the middle of our part of the program, and I became aware of some sort of disturbance on the last tier of risers. I was shocked to hear Bill's voice. He had disobeyed the principal and sneaked in the backstage door. He had determinedly and forcibly removed his substitute, taken his place, and said his lines. After the last number, I went backstage to find him, and he was waiting for me. His words were,"Those are my lines, and nobody's going to take them away from me."

The principal and I considered his punishment, felt that something rather miraculous had happened, and made his school community service another social experience. Bill became a positive member of his society and a valuable part of the speech choir. Later, he began a career in radio announcing. He found his identity from the rewards of participating with others in a worthwhile experience.

The students and I could not have achieved what we did with any other medium of expression because choric utterance requires individual sensing of universal truths, preserving individualized expression while creating a powerful speaking force for those ideas and feelings that are communal and universal in nature. No individual can express such emotions; since the feelings are those of humanity, it takes humanity to say them. One person trying to say such words turns them into propaganda; choric speaking of these feelings makes them mine and yours—utterances of humankind since time began. This was what I wanted my students to feel as they merged their individual strengths with others to effect a totality of feeling, of interpretation, of projection to an audience. This made each one both a "me" and "we"— a person and a part of history, past, present, and future. The adolescent, without analyzing or even understanding his or her "solitary state," begins, in the unity of humanity's commonly shared emotions and ideas, to feel that he or she is not really alone—all of humanity has been there before.

Thus, in this period of my life, I was imagining what is possible, what *can* be good and right, seeking for something old, yet new, where the students and I could walk down the same path together. I felt that choric drama provided what I considered to be the *best* possibility for the finding of identity. We each had individual purposes and individual expectancies and were developing and growing in personal talents, values, insights, and convictions; but we simultaneously gained in appreciation of the wonderful world of differences,

This was not our sole drama experience, for there are many other forms of dramatic experience which expand the horizons and deepen our roots, but choric utterance brought a new dimension into our dramatic studies, and it did something especially valuable for all of us. It led me to discover and participate in a new form of theater—to grow older innovatively and creatively; but the sharing with adolescents in their search for identity added new and fascinating perceptions and insights, invaluable to me as a person. I was discovering new motivations, new resources I didn't know *I* had.

My yearnings for the pink dress are shared by humanity from time immemorial when limitations kept individuals or nations from attaining their desires for something not possessed and desperately wished for: a homeland, the stability of a secure position and career, serenity amid the conflict and confusion of displacement, a faith to undergird insecurities, tangible proof of prestige and approval—these are but a few longings.

There were many changes of residence for us, as with many parsonage people, but wherever my father's Bible and my mother's silver candlesticks were was home for us. In the years following childhood, something always seemed to be helping me to put down roots wherever I was, to find a basic inner sense of security within constant change.

All adolescents seek a true identity, not just a veneer of identification and imitation. Role models are vitally important, and those who offer something worthy and honorable afford a foundation that offers permanent value. In much of the literature learned in the choric speaking, the adolescents met great people, great minds and hearts, great thoughts, and they, too, sought the "high ground" as preferable to the inferior standards so destructive of future aspirations and hopes.

Youth might ask, chorically, "Why don't our elders understand us? How can we talk to people who don't remember that they, too, were once young as we are?" Uttered by one voice the speaker seems to be complaining, criticizing those who are older. Together, their voices are an orchestra, playing their own music as they compose it to match their special yearnings.

When we read the choric lament of the Trojan women who lived centuries ago, we hear the shrieking agony of displaced persons today, of the dispossessed and homeless in our own cities and countries, of an entire generation of "The Lost Children," who are the products of war, of hunger, of disease. We should be able to hear the voices of our first Americans, the Cherokee nation, driven from their mountain home to a distant home in the West, with thousands of them dying on a trek called the Cherokee "Trail of Tears."

When some element of the human condition is chorically uttered, I see and sense the feelings of an entire people, and I am part of it. I am expanding my horizons and my sympathies. Individually spoken I may not accept what is being said. I may rationalize, "Oh, well, that was just one person," and I can shrug it off. I take notice, however, of many voices speaking the same message. Universal utterance creates a force not to be denied.

At eighty-five, I rejoice that I learned, with my students, to join the great caravan of this human search for identity; for age, while making solitude seem natural, does not necessarily create loneliness. Loneliness is of the spirit; choric utterance took me into history and made me an heir of its greatness.

In reliving some moments in my eighty-five years, I know that not every event has been remembered. Some have been lost, either because they did not register or because time has erased them from my memory for now. But all that life has been to me has brought me to this time and place, and in ways I may not understand, has prepared me, well or poorly, for the fascinating and engrossing process of growing old.

Rearview Mirror

One more look backward: Once when I was traveling in the highest region of the Alps, I was so concentrated upon the precipitous winding hairpin road and the frightening dropoffs into the unseen depths far below that I, like the others on the bus, was gripping the back of the seat in front of me so tightly that my knuckles were white from the pressure. Our bodies were stiff with tension. We did not see anything else but the road, and we did not care about what we were supposed to be seeing along the way. We barely spoke, not only because we did not want to distract the driver, but most of us lacked the breath to utter words other than little shrieks or moans. Just when the strain was becoming unendurable, our driver cheerfully called out, "We'll pull off just ahead for a brief stop."

We thought he was crazy, but he knew the road and knew where he was, and this was the one place where a wide overlook permitted a bus stop. We all trembled out to stand upon firm ground, and we saw a sign that, translated, means, Now look back and see where you have been.

The scene for miles was magnificent and one of awe-inspiring grandeur and beauty beyond description. We just stood there in silence to look and feel. It is that beauty and magnificence that I remember today, and we broke into song that matched the feeling we had: "How Great Thou Art." It was a deeply spiritual moment, an experience that reminds me over and over again to look back to see where I have been, and from there, to think about where I am going.

The events that taught me how to be eighty-three, eighty-four, eighty-five, and beyond—possessed a value that I couldn't possibly perceive at the time they happened. Now I know that at age five I needed to learn to accept change as the essence of life and of growth and that my reactions to that change would make the difference for me between self-acceptance or self-rejection.

Learning at age seven who I was and later choosing what I would be called established me to myself as a person possessed of identity; it also confirmed my sense of belonging. I need to know this at eighty-five, for knowing who I am affords me the basis for my status as an individual and as part of a totality to which I make my personal contribution, and from which I receive recognition as part of the whole.

Those robin's-egg blue walls ruined by large blobs of glued-on pamphlet paper taught me to respect property belonging to others. Throughout the years my understanding of this concept has grown to help me respect the rights of others to express different ideas, to have different religious and political beliefs, to enjoy different music, and to feel differently about the world. I learned to respect persons because of the differences that allow us to mutually enrich one another's lives. This was not an easy lesson to learn, because personal security is at risk when someone with a different view is right, but my understanding started in the blue room and was reinforced by Judge Hyatt in a living history class years later.

I experienced the solace and companionship of prayer when the pink dress became so important to me, for, in pleading for the dress, I talked to the Almighty as I would have spoken to my parents, depending upon God's love for me to give me a fair hearing. When my prayer was answered, I learned that others were often instruments of God's will. Prayer became for me as natural as breathing, and how my prayers were answered led me to evaluate my prayer life as to its power or its inadequacy. I even found there were times when I just couldn't pray at all, and Etta Baldwin Oldham's lines gave me the comfort of knowing that I wasn't alone in this failure:

> Jis' Blue, God,
> Jis' blue.
> Ain't prayin' exactly jis' now
> > tear blind, I guess,
> > cain't see my way through . . . .
> And you said, Ast, . . .
> > Somehow I ain't astin' now,
> > And I hardly know whut to do.
> Hope jis' sorter left,
> but Faith's still here,—
> > Faith ain't gone too . . . .
> > . . . I ain't doubtin' you,
> But I ain't prayin' to-night, God—
> > Jis' blue.[2]

When I felt this way and sensed my own inadequacy, somehow I always felt that God's presence was there within the shadows keeping watch above his own. I certainly learned to depend upon prayer not only to get what I wanted, but to strengthen my relationship with my

Creator. I also learned that prayers are not always answered in my way but that keeping the communication lines open assures me of a listening ear and a love that perpetually guides and guards me. At eighty-five, this is my greatest possession.

At eighty-five, I am aware of what my students meant to my life. We traveled many roads together, they at their pace and I at mine, each seeking our individual ways of expressing ideas and feelings. Their curiosity and search for answers were strong motivations for me to discover how to open up for them greener pastures and wider horizons to excite their creative pursuits. In searching how to lead them into self-discovery, I learned more about my own needs and possibilities.

Humor was always in and around events in the parsonage, for there were times of grim reality, of lack of what we call the necessities of life, of wondering how we would manage from one day to the next. However, the objectivity that humor injects into a situation helped us to reduce the emotionalism that could cloud our management of the situation and enabled us to talk together, to consider possible alternatives, or just to grin and bear it—together. The day my father was thrown headlong into the Laughing Mule Saloon could have made him the laughingstock of that little western community; but when he kept his sense of humor and challenged Dallas Eicherhorn to keep his word and come to church, my father took advantage of a golden opportunity and not only won Dallas without an argument, but made a place of affectionate respect for himself in the hearts of the townspeople. The twinkle in my father's eyes won many a decision for a divided congregation and soothed the troubled waters as to who would sing the solo in the choir.

At eighty-five, I am privileged to be experiencing oldness at this particular time and place in history. As one writer suggested, "If you're going to be old, now is the time to do it!" A newer world can be envisioned and brought into being by the elders. With their experience and with their varied and highly individual abilities and knowledge, they know how to work miracles, and their numbers give them the power to do anything they want or need to do. Do they have the will to bring about the greatness and the goodness so long desired and not yet achieved? What will they do with their moment of destiny? Who knows? This has never happened before, but what is certain is that the elders will determine the moral quality of the next century and will determine the future for the future. We have fifty years for our moment, and this is our only time. Will we make a difference, and if so, what kind of difference? What kind of a world do we hope for? How do we make this happen? Are we that generation standing on a tiptoe of expectation, a people chosen to accomplish a particular purpose? Or will we lose our chance and leave it to someone else to be the architect of a perfection imagined but yet to be made reality? Time will tell, but believing that it is not by chance that we are a people here in such numbers for a once-in-history appearance, that there is a meaning in our presence, let us paraphrase Longfellow: Let us, then, be up and doing, With a heart for any fate; Still achieving, still pursuing, learn to labor and not to wait.

Oldness puts me in an aging society at this unparalleled time, and affords me this rare historical opportunity to share in a unique human experience. Looking back to see where I have been, I find myself in a great company of those delegated to make a newer and better world. All of us are collectors of highly individualized life packets never to be duplicated. When we search our own life attic, we find moments that bring back memories of both delight and pain. Do you remember when . . . is the start of a trip that spans the years and gives life its continuity.

Being eighty-five means making age work for me, not against me. For too long, humanity has viewed age as an enemy, hostile to us, and many have used up their time in vain attempts to hold fast to fantasy youth. Perhaps it is our inherent longing to live forever, for as one man said, I'm sure of what's happening to me here; somewhere else, who knows? Perhaps it is fear of the unknown, even when our known is far from perfect, maybe even unendurable; or perhaps, it is our yearning to experience more of a world that we have enjoyed. Perhaps we feel as did Edna St. Vincent Millay, O world, I cannot hold thee close enough!

But whatever it is that makes us cling to youth and deny the normalcy of age, with me now at eighty-five it is the *now* that counts. I look on aging as the gift of life, and it is built into the divine plan of creation. History is certainly going somewhere, and we are either in the way of it or on the way with it. If it is the latter, then there is much to be accomplished. In the next part of this book, a preview of the great tasks awaiting us, the elders, is set in a periphery of moral and ethical issues, and we, the Larger Generation, will determine policies and decisions affecting our total society. The tasks—and the will to accomplish them—may very well bring about much inner conflict.

Making any decision based on moral values of what is right and good causes us to struggle as we attempt to settle the situation in a strange setting, far removed from the times in which we were reared, and for a time in which we have never lived.

Forty years ago Henry Commager posed some ponderous questions. Do they sound familiar? He pointed out that Americans had established the highest standard of living known in history; how would they continue to live? Theirs was an economy of abundance; would they develop a fair distribution of that abundance? They were using up their natural resources faster than they were replacing them; would science reverse the process or would resources cease to satisfy the need? From what had been an almost classless society, would inequalities of wealth develop divisions of haves and have nots? They had the largest educational system in the world, but for what would it educate? With more leisure than any other Western people, what would they do with it? They had all but eliminated God from their affairs, but what or whom would they put in God's place? They possessed intelligence, but would their intelligence help them find solutions for their future complexities? Having made the atomic bomb, how would they use its power—for the benefit or destruction of civilization? The whole world had an interest in the answers which history would make to these questions.[3]

Do you get the feeling, as I do, that these mind-boggling problems that faced us in 1950 and before are facing us today and are worsening? Perhaps, almost certainly, history has been waiting for us, the Larger Generation, to appear just at this time to find solutions. Thus, I am looking back only to look ahead to the testing of our minds and souls. Will we dare to take on the future?

PART TWO

THE AGE OF GERONTOCRACY:
A Call to Action

America is striving desperately and urgently to rediscover, reaffirm, and reestablish its moral and ethical foundations, lost in recent years to the uncertainties of expediency, compromise, personal selfishness, and corporate greed.

Some issues seem to dare humanity to do its best, but to expect failure.

Other issues seem to say, "Look at me! Things are bad, but not impossible. Use your imagination, look for what is not there, but what could be with vision and confidence. Have the will and the courage to try!"

The next two chapters confront issues crucial to the next fifty years and beyond. These issues must be met head on with the determination to find effective answers. Some issues will be more difficult than others. But all are part of our Age of Gerontocracy, and our legacy to the future must be a better world—more humane, kinder, more compassionate, and closer to the realization of God's kingdom on this earth.

> But I have promises to keep,
> And miles to go before I sleep . . .
> —Robert Frost

We must be on our way, for the world—and history—are waiting.

8.
Making a Career Out of Aging:
Issues That Dare Us to Fail

I remember when I said out loud to myself, "You're old!" I do not recall the exact date, but I remember the event vividly. In retrospect, I believe that I uttered my declaration of independence in defiance of a television commercial that I had just heard in which someone had exclaimed that she was not old, was not going to be old, and, in short, seemed to be promising to live forever. I was indignant at her denial of an inevitable reality, and I said to the commercial, "You're so busy trying to recapture the fantasy of youth that you're wasting the reality of age and the life it has given you!"

When I went to the mirror, looked myself straight in the eye, and said, "I'm old!" it became real. But the corners of my mouth were turned down, and my frown was grim and joyless. Those two words went downhill all the way to the bottom. Then I said it again; my eyes gleamed, the corners of my mouth turned up in a wide grin, and my voice rang out as if in a proud declaration. That day I learned something important to my being eighty-five—for "oldness" is very special and very precious; it is not to be denied. We have to make age work for us; we can't treat it as an enemy.

This chapter challenges us to face the realities of a society privileged to have available great numbers of experienced persons, diverse in achievements and abilities. This rare combination offers a genuine dare—a dare to be creative catalysts for change, a dare to discover, develop, and design a society that reaps vast benefits from the constructive involvement of this aging force. To fail to utilize these untapped resources is to have a stagnant, static, and unproductive Age of Gerontocracy; older adults would simply be marking time while progress passes us by. Solutions simply must be found for some issues, and the solvers are the Larger Generation from now until 2030-2040. We must view the responsibility as our opportunity in history to make great things happen—to cause impossibilities to become possibilities!

I make no claims to prophecy, but I look ahead to the unpredictable crises and the soothing tranquilities of the years ahead. International restructurings have erased familiar relationships, and rising uncertainties in domestic situations shake us loose from moorings we have long felt were there. There are so many things to be done, so many new discoveries to make:

    —varying adventures in learning, new realities of day-to-day living to face and to tackle;

    —changes to expect and to welcome, some to avoid;

    —a new "me" to take time to get reacquainted with at a scheduled time on my calendar;

    —another birthday to celebrate with thanksgiving and rejoicing;

    —times to test a sense of humor to see if I can still laugh at myself as well as with others;

    —moments to recognize that only prayer can bring comfort and guidance for a situation beyond my control;

    —opportunities to challenge a prejudice with information that destroys that prejudice;

    —evidences of a faith justified to give new strength to a personal faith;

    —potential disasters to be confronted with a belief that there is a solution and that this is a test for my problem-solving abilities;

    —an adverse result to be turned into an advantage;

    —a new sense of belonging, and with it, an increasing sense of responsibility for those who do *not* belong;

    —something dreamed of and wished for made possible through personal effort and the support of others;

    —the discovery of unexpected skill in coping;

    —opportunities to continue to learn and to experience how to become what I potentially am able to become;

    —ability to use my "staying power" to seize every moment, making time my partner in a re-engagement with life, a re-investment of myself in life.

    What next? How do we avoid failure to meet these opportunities? We see troublesome question marks in our tomorrows. What will we, the elders, do with a tomorrow that is ours to control? What do we need to do to turn our wisdom, talents, experience, and values into assets for a greatness never before experienced? Where will we get the information required for intelligent action? From where will we find the counseling and guidance, the courage, and the spiritual strength to seize the opportunities and make things happen for good? What happens when the individual is trapped in his or her own value system, inherited from a past that has little if any relationship with the present or to a future affected by a decision? Trying to reach a solution can tear a person apart, especially if that solution involves moral or ethical issues—and most issues awaiting us in our tomorrow will be of that nature. Our tomorrow will be a time when "what is right" becomes a choice based on the individual's interpretation of what is right. Then we fail when bias dictates the decision, and its action has far-reaching effects upon the lives of others.

Happily, the resources are vast: information is expanding, almost too rapidly for most of us to keep up with it or to understand much of it. But as we draw upon community resources, become part of a communication network, get on mailing lists of elected officials and of organizations for the aging, we set up a pattern of information from credible sources. With conferences, workshops, and community authorities and agencies and with the pursuit of personal interests and common concerns, we can find a whole world of knowledge and expertise just asking to be used. Discussions bring about a sharing of ignorance that at least creates a fellowship of wondering, and wondering is the beginning of knowledge. An inexhaustible reservoir of information waits for our exploration.

When the younger generations, with their firsthand knowledge of their times and concerns add their experience to those of the Larger Generation, we meld a joint heritage that offers great promise. The moral issues in our future must have solutions, and the persons with experience happen to be here to find the answers. For each of the issues discussed in this chapter (and for other problems), we must keep before us as a measuring rod these questions: If we fail to find a solution, what then is the result? What alternative is there? And what is the effect upon humanity?

Income. Since Social Security is the major source of income for most of the older citizens, it is basic to the survival and dignity of these elders. Sixty-two percent of older persons receive one-half of their total income from Social Security; twenty-four percent rely on it for at least ninety percent of their income; and fourteen percent of these aged beneficiaries obtain *all* of their income from Social Security.[4] Furthermore, this Larger Generation of elders must use this income not only for their own maintenance, but also for the financial support of every aspect of their society. Thus, with seventy to ninety million persons over age fifty-five in the coming century, the economy will be in their hands as consumers and as producers, and their actions will determine our economic future.

Pensions, health costs, especially health insurance, housing, and discriminatory employment practices all require serious and constant scrutiny by the elderly policy makers who have accurate, credible sources to guide their decisions. An informed and highly motivated advocacy is essential to ensure effective action and to protect against exploitation through misinformation. Consumer education is a "must."

In its current form, the Consumer Price Index (CPI) does not match the circumstances of the older American; yet, it is to this data that the very important COLA (Cost of Living Adjustment) to Social Security is bound. The *AARP Bulletin* (October, 1989) (American Association For Retired Persons) headlined this moral issue: "America's Oldest Old Need a Raise." This is a moral issue because the only raise that Social Security recipients ever receive is the COLA, which is a yearly slight increase in recognition of inflation and is already a year in arrears. The present CPI is based in a survey that *did not include any retired person,* and the survey reports data relating to the spending patterns of urban wage earners and clerical workers (who make up about thirty-two percent of the population), whose spending patterns are far different from those of older citizens whose COLA is tied to this survey. One former senator who caught this inequality of treatment called this situation "inflation without representation."[5] Income is always going to be a deep concern of many elders and their families and communities. Monitoring legislation and being intelligently involved in legislative advocacy is a necessity in the coming century.

The Minority Elderly. Related to the income issue is the issue of the minority elderly who become a challenge and an opportunity. It is projected that there will be a 283 percent increase in this population in the next fifty years, with Hispanics increasing five times faster than non-Hispanics.[6] In such increases in population of minority elderly, there is always the potential risk of overlooking the legislative dimensions—that the tribal grantees have increased, but that a corresponding funding to provide for this increase in needs has failed to be requested. Thus, basic necessities to ensure survival and human dignity are lacking, a crisis arises, and it is too late for the many who cannot wait for another time. For society, this failure is critical as an economic issue and as a social moral requisite. Guilt confronts us when there is clear conflict between our national statements of purpose as a people and our fulfillment of that purpose. Learning to be eighty-five has given me a new awareness of what it really means to be a "part of all that I have met." Ignorance or apathy which causes neglect and suffering, even death, to any of our citizens is a fault which the conscience cannot endure.

Failure to provide adequate Social Security benefits is to risk economic disaster. For example, Social Security is our largest social program, and it is not a *charity* program—it is an "earned rights" program. Its cash flow into the national economy is a dependable factor in the economy. Without Social Security as a "pay-as-you-go" program enabling persons to plan for some degree of independence in their later years, the alternatives are too grim to consider. Welfare and absolute charity would drain the national treasury and undermine the dignity of older Americans or leave the dependent elders resourceless. Neither of these alternatives deserves any consideration as a *moral* possibility. A vigilant Larger Generation that become the policy makers must be ever alert, informed, and moved to remedy inequalities and injustice in the system. Older persons must work toward the immediate goal of having Social Security safely established in its own trust fund, protected from raiding and from borrowing. For Social Security is an *earned income* fund—it belongs only to those who worked throughout their lives and "paid as they went" throughout their working years. It is a contract between a government and its people. At eighty-five, I feel a deep sense of obligation to keep credibly informed and to act responsibly in legislative advocacy. And so must we all as we are dared to fail.

Stewardship of Our Environment. This is a vitally important moral issue that, if we are not to fail, demands our utmost attention, lest our own lives, as well as that of generations to come, be severely at risk. Pure water, clean air, productive soil, and safe deposit of hazardous waste are urgent priorities. We cannot afford the luxury of delay. The information we need is there for the asking. Becoming politically educated and involved in electing candidates who will make the environment a major goal can serve the electorate's interests in a real way.

Health. For many older persons, income maintenance and health become closely related issues. Some health considerations facing the policy makers in the Age of Gerontocracy have far-reaching moral implications and may well cause personal conflicts for many. Biases arising from past experiences, especially those based in religious convictions (such as organ transplants and life-support systems), may contravene factual information and a necessity to act for preservation of life. Trapped in the conflict, a policy maker may find himself or herself facing conscience-troubling emotions and subsequent guilt. The medical profession is facing new and searching questions. A "living will," recognized in most states, eliminates much confusion later when the intent of the patient cannot be understood and family members are divided. A living will is advisable, and many physicians welcome it. Elders should make their friends and family aware of the existence of a living will and should include in it specifics that will ensure that their wishes are followed.

Policy makers will be making momentous decisions about moral questions such as these: What obligations does society have for the health care of the poor, aged, and young? Is health care a right or a privilege? What moral issues are inherent in the rapid advance in genetic experimentation? What right do individuals have to choose their own time and method of dying, and how did the Supreme Court decision of June 1990, nationalizing a limited right to die, affect this matter?

A newspaper published by the American Society on Aging asked in a front-page article, "Is It Time for Euthanasia?" The story stated that, because of the importance of personal choice in dying, older—and younger—citizens in California had launched a campaign to secure enough names on a petition for placing this issue on the state ballot in November 1988. The legislation was titled Human and Dignified Death Act (HDDA) Initiative and would make it legal for a physician to help a terminally ill patient die at a time and in the manner of his or her own choosing.

This initiative for an active euthanasia measure failed on its way to the ballot box because only 289,000 of the 372,000 signatures required to qualify for the ballot were secured, but the interesting thing is that the issue of euthanasia came this close in 1988. A few years ago, such action would not have been contemplated, certainly not activated for legislative action. But as thousands watched their spouses suffer through agonizing months while bills piled up, or as they contemplated a prolonged, miserable dying, it is not surprising, perhaps, that the public reacted to its fear of pain and suffering by legalizing the writing of a directive that would enable the terminally ill to experience a humane dying where the patient's comfort and dignity are the priorities. The Age of Gerontocracy must find ways to usher people out of life as happily as we welcome most of them into life.

So when do you pull the plug? How do you select recipients for organ transplants? How are these transplants paid for? What do you do in a shortfall of organ donors? In the delivery of health care, is such care *available for all, affordable for all, accessible for all, and accountable to all?* If not, then there is a rationing of our health care, making it more difficult, if not impossible, for many to benefit from the system. Is health care for wellness (prevention) of parallel importance with remedial health care? Can home health care be effective, financially and psychologically, when a home is not constructed for such measures, and when the caregiver is untrained and under stress?

The health issue of long-term care is easily the first priority with many older Americans. In a person's lifetime, long-term care is a normal expectation that is already growing far beyond the financial reach of most people. Its devastating effect upon the financial security of older citizens and their families makes paupers and charity recipients of those who must spend all that they have saved. They end up surrendering their dignity along with their money to pay for the costs of such care, *if* they can get it. The cost of long-term care insurance is not only very expensive, but it is not available after a certain age, and policies differ as to what they offer. Entire families become hostages to poverty in caring for their frail and elderly, and they leave themselves open to charity in their own later years. Supplementary insurance, a stopgap, may or may not serve the person's need at any one time, and changes in Medicare and Medicaid make for insecurity and anxiety. To fail in finding rational solutions to this moral issue will result in hardship, even death, for many of our citizens.

Our health system reflects a jumble of conflicting assumptions, priorities, and choices; the present "turf protection" causes duplication of money, energy, and resources with a consequent confusion in the public's mind. And we have not yet developed a system to match our society's values and expectations. Divergencies among the states do show some strong, innovative programs *for some states,* but others may omit entire areas of need and take no legislative action to correct deficiencies. "Underachieving" states cause divergencies that create discriminatory treatment of citizens and present a threat to the common good; for what threatens one, threatens all.

Diversity in health care legislation, while encouraging individuality and initiative by separate states, may put our nation at risk. Research to prevent epidemics such as AIDS must become a basic part of national survival and continued good health. A health program designed for our own national protection is an issue demanding immediate and continuing action, and these policies will confront our elderly policy makers throughout the Age of Gerontocracy. What a legacy our elders could leave with a health care plan that offers the protection of a guaranteed base of support and security for our nation's good health! Failure to realize the moral context of this issue and to confront it courageously and with vision is to invite national disaster.

As Employees and Consumers. Rethinking and restructuring of work as it affects the older worker and the economy of his or her society dares us to fail because the older adults will *be* the economy in the next century—as worker and as consumer. For example, Social Security and its billions of dollars in earned rights income puts back into the economy those same billions of dollars almost immediately after retired persons receive them.

As consumers, our numbers create the marketplace, and the demand to please the older buyer who will be the major earner and spender in the Age of Gerontocracy will necessitate many changes. In the health area, consider what a difference it will make when seventy percent of patients in a doctor's office are over sixty! It will not be acceptable for a doctor to rationalize to an elderly patient that, because one knee hurts, it is because the patient is the age of seventy or eighty. The older patient knows that the other knee is the same age, and it isn't hurting. So, when age is not the reason for a difficulty, the real cause of the problem, and a remedy, may be found. The Age of Gerontocracy will require better answers, and these answers may not only solve the immediate problems, but may lead to a discovery of how to prevent the same problems from affecting those who follow.

The clothing industry will find it necessary to design for older men and women. The entertainment field will find that its principal source of income is from those who dance to less spine-breaking rhythms; the food industry will bring to the shelves products related to aging needs and tastes and will have to provide nutritious packaged food for the single eater; transportation will be revolutionized if it is to function for an aging population; housing will focus upon safety, beauty, convenience, and location in relation to needed buying centers; and neighborhoods free from crime become a necessity. All these and more will be expected in response to the expanding older populations whose needs and numbers make the demands essential.

Older people, needing to supplement their income, become a great untapped reservoir of knowledge, skill, and expertise. Innovative employment options utilize present abilities and the learning of new skills—ones that need immediate attention. The older worker's expertise is irreplaceable, and the waste of it deserves serious scrutiny.

Magnetizing the great productive resources of the older experienced persons will mean the injection of unexplored and undeveloped potential into our economic life. As the major work force, the older workers bring a wealth of expertise, skills, and knowledge; they are work-oriented, and their attitudes and interest in their work as well as genuine concern for the quality of their efforts commend them to any employer.

Policy makers must consider older workers when they wrestle with difficult economic issues. For example, "downsizing" deprives older workers and the corporate ranks when consolidations, buyouts, mergers, restructuring, and foreign competition cost the worker a job. Since many of these jobs are those of experienced, managerial, and professional levels, where will industry and business go for leadership in managerial and entrepreneurial activity if the older worker has been phased out? These people are essential to carry on production, but, even more important, they provide ideas and vision.

Some early retirement plans are called the "Golden Boot"—an "offer you cannot refuse." Often, incentives are offered to some, not to others, and sometimes the offer is accompanied by an intimidating unspoken threat that if the worker rejects the retirement plan offered, he or she is vulnerable to future layoffs when the early retirement plan is no longer in effect. The business world needs to be alert *now* that the Age of Gerontocracy will bring a new stimulus for economic growth in the next century. With the decrease in younger workers—a demographic fact—the older worker becomes a major resource, and there is no substitute for that worker's experience.

The Baby Boom generation has provided employers with a plentiful supply of experienced workers. But the Baby Bust generation following the boom promises employers a diminished supply of young entrants to the labor force, especially in managerial positions where voluntary or enforced retirement has drained off the expertise of older, more experienced people.[7] (This situation is frighteningly apparent to such professions as teaching and medical technicians where years of preparation are necessary.)

By the year 2000, the work force will be forty-seven percent female and almost two-thirds of the new employees will be women. But with women as a major part of the work force, problems of elder and child care will intensify, and the average woman—the chief caregiver—can expect to spend eighteen years caring for an elderly family member and seventeen years caring for children. Since these obligations do not usually occur simultaneously, the caregiving responsibilities require about thirty-five years of a caregiver's most productive and creative years, eroding many personal self-enriching or career opportunities. For the older woman, this is a role overload during her most vulnerable time of life. Failure to solve this issue is to endanger the economy, but, more importantly, to place at hazard the health and personal development of those women carrying two heavily-loaded responsibilities. The answer would seem to lie in discovering and designing an economy to match the older worker—to evaluate the person's talent and ability and to find ways to match this with society's needs. We now do it the other way around—fit a person into some predetermined economic requirement, often not to the greatest good. This is the time for new thoughts and imaginative planning, and it is the elders who must respond.

A survey of managers and supervisors indicated that job performance was down, productivity decreased, and work quality suffered among caregivers. Eleven percent of the female work force have to quit work to become caregivers, and their health, financial security, and creative contributions to their world are at risk. Seventy-five percent of the managers in the survey reported unscheduled time off by caregivers; seventy-three percent listed lateness; sixty-seven percent cited absenteeism, and sixty-four percent gave excessive telephone usage as reasons for the lack of quality in work by caregivers. Thus caregiving is integrally related to our economic future, and "elder care becomes the number one work place issue of the 1990's."[8]

In chapter nine, other crucial issues based in moral values will focus on Tennyson's exhortation:

> *Come, my friends,*
> *'Tis not too late*
> *To seek a newer world.*

Implicit in these words is the dare to do it. It's your time, you are here. Dare to create a goodness and a greatness such as the world has never experienced. Do it!

We must create hope for a world that sees bleakness. In the summer of 1990, a special summer school experience was offered to a selected group of students in one school system. One of the students' concluding assignments in this creative writing course was to write about the world they envision when they are forty years of age. Their perceptiveness was amazing, and their understanding of the present made clear what our Age of Gerontocracy must do, for they would be a part of our age, too. Here is what one girl wrote, and we, the elders, are the ones to whom she is really writing.

> Crime is still at large, disease is still a plague, and the homeless are still without a home. Pollution is still hovering over our heads, drugs are still on the streets . . .
>
> Although life on earth is an empire of advanced technology, it is a world of greed, suffering, pollution, drugs and crime just as it was forty years ago. We don't give a serious thought to the homeless, starvation, pollution, and other problems. We don't have enough time. We went on to make life the way it was—the same.[9]

A student in another class wrote a similar thought: "Why didn't I understand what was happening? Why didn't *we* do something about what was wrong? I guess you have to grow up before you realize what you didn't understand when you were young!"

As we face the future, we must confront aspects of our world and times that cry out for remedies before it is too late. These issues strike at the very roots of survival and of human dignity, and at the progress of our race against time in establishing moral and ethical values as the heart of our culture. In Chapter nine, several issues, potentially destructive to these values, present the challenge to succeed in producing a Utopian future, a magnificent possibility, where goodness and greatness run like a mighty current under, around, and within our societal actions to create a significant moment in history that we call the Age of Gerontocracy.

9.
A Charge to Keep I Have:
Issues That Dare Us to Succeed

Chapter eight proposed crucial issues that challenged us. This chapter introduces additional issues for which we must search and find solutions that could bring into reality more humaneness, greater compassion, and more generous understanding of and respect for the value of our differences.

A few issues belong in both chapters, but with different emphases upon the results of their failure or of their success. Embracing all of the issues is that potentially powerful force—the Age of Gerontocracy with the unique opportunity that it offers for achievement. Here, for only fifty years, as a combination of numbers and experience, the elders have their hour upon the stage. This must be the time of productive creativity, of values achieved, of a new role in a new era, of a new concept of human worth and dignity, and a new vision of a purpose indigenous to elderhood.

There is no guarantee of what will happen; a new greatness can permeate our world, or apathy and "I'll sit this one out" can produce a "retired" world. If the latter results, not only will our society pay the penalty, but the elders themselves go on "standby" for the final and most rewarding years of their lives.

We have always seemed to place a high value on antiques—antique furniture, antique houses, antique jewelry—but we are just beginning to recognize the pricelessness of antique people; their oldness is invaluable and irreplaceable, and they are our nation's most valuable human resource.

The word *retirement* should be eliminated from the vocabulary of our people because of the attitude it breeds. A prominent physician remarked once that it is a killer word, for essentially, it encourages an attitude of secession from engagement with life and sidelines so many from activities and participation in a life of growth and achievement. *Reinvestment* or *reengagement*—even *recycling*—give better images of a cycle of self-realization, a stimulating excitement and purpose in learning in every aspect of one's being. Reinvestment puts back into the world what life has taught, benefiting others, especially those who follow. Perhaps the greatest ethical concern now should be the creation of a new image of the older persons—to equip them for their new role—initiating and directing leadership of their world. They are, numerically, going to be the motivating power; it follows that this power must be projected into decisive and informed action by a people empowered for this responsibility. A continued reinforcement of dependence and of retreat from a dynamic utilization of the experience that age has given would seem to be not only a liability, but a moral and ethical injustice, depriving older persons of achievement and realization of their personal goals.

In the years ahead, sixty-five will not be old; the ages of fifty-five to sixty-four will be the "golden years" wherein to plan for the third of life that is still waiting. What will the world do with us? The accent is upon the *with*. For the power rests in the numbers, and this new age is one shaped by the predominance of the older generation. It will constantly restructure itself and will often place the policy makers in conscience-troubling conflicts as they come to grips with matters of far-reaching import as well as of immediate concern. The decision makers may well be caught in a quandary between what is right to them and what is expedient for public policy; their experience is in a past, and their policies and decisions affect a present and a future for which their knowledge and attitudes may not prepare them. And so they ask: "How do I deal with this? I need information, advice, guidance, education!"

Certain societal factors affecting the actions of the elderly policy makers arise out of our time and place in history. We should, before listing these factors, ask a penetrating question: Is age morally relevant, anyway? Our response can be yes if we recognize that the older persons and their society have perpetuated a stereotype of age as a time to move over, to retire. The new role for elders has to be one of responsive and responsible leadership as older persons are seen as initiators, activators, participators, idea generators, contributors, and donors. This will become the acceptable and expected behavior.

The stereotype of "get off the stage and let others take over" has caused a criminal waste of priceless ability needed by each succeeding generation. The development of a new "stereotype" for elders is being inhibited by the attitudes of our society—including the elders. This self-perpetuating cycle will not end until change is brought about concerning the following issues:

1. Failure to comprehend the new age and the new role, its characters, and its demands.

2. Lack of motivation; a reinforcement through habit; lack of adequate information and preparation for a new role, especially in legislative advocacy; an attitude of "I've served my time."

3. Existence of special interest groups—a splintering of society into competitive actions; "turf protection" to the detriment of unity of purpose for common goals (especially in seeking funds).

4. Political exploitation.

5. Ignorance and apathy.

6. Misuse of the power residing in the numbers of the older populations.

7. Feminization of society.

8. Need for continuing education about this expanding world that the elderly will control and direct; education in advocacy based in moral and ethical practices.

9. Ability to analyze media presentations and the impact of them upon the public's rights to access honest information and accurate representation of facts relating to candidates and issues that will determine their future.

Issues that dare us to succeed present a challenge to dare and do with courage and vision, for where there is no vision, the people perish. If we fail in this, the Age of Gerontocracy loses its focus, its chance to initiate a new era.

Self-determination and Autonomy or, negatively, the reinforcement of dependency. Dr. Terrie Wetele, in a speech given at Harvard Medical School, emphasized that the autonomy of the individual is a basic human value; the individual has the right to make decisions that are voluntary and intentional, not the result of coercion, duress, or undue influence. But individual decisions are not truly autonomous because of constraints placed by available choices, by the person's own strengths and weaknesses, and by the wishes of others. Cognitive ability and individual functioning are variables in decision making.

Sometimes when autonomy is lost or taken away, "paternalism" is frequently practiced with the best of intentions, and interference with a person's liberty of action is justified by reasons based in the good, the happiness, the needs, or the interests of the person being coerced. But whatever the justification, lacking the right to choose reinforces a sense of low esteem and enhances the state of dependence, lessening or destroying completely any motivation for self-realization or societal participation.

Reinforcement of dependence or independence thus is basic to survival and dignity and directs one to an attitude toward life itself. Independence, which is a lifelong goal, begins to wane with a limited participation in an active life; and with this, a sense of self-esteem, value, and achievement vanishes. An early identity—"I know who I am and whatever happens to me at any age is a reality with which a 'real me' can deal"—is essential for the later years when invidious comparison with earlier, more attractive years, betrays us into denying our oldness and its growing dependence on others. But physical dependence does not necessarily mean surrender of an individual's right to choice, to participation in the society that needs the experience and knowledge that he or she possesses. Until the end of this life, a person must be needed—and must know it!

Guardianship. In legal situations, such as that of guardianship and custodial supervision, the question of the civil rights of the ward becomes critical. Barring a stroke or a heart attack that suddenly puts an end to life, all of us at some time will confront the need for guardian care, either for ourselves or as guardian for someone else. The House Committee on Aging has called the guardianship situation a national disgrace, and *Money* magazine described the problem in a lengthy article "The Gulag of Guardianship." Since 500,000 Americans are now denied the right to exercise control over their lives and their property when declared incompetent, and since the next fifty years will see the number of those needing assistance doubled, it is clear that society's dilemma will be how to guarantee the necessary protection to these people without infringing on the individual's private and personal rights.

Perhaps the greatest moral question is how to enable a person to remain actively involved as a contributing citizen to a society that still needs what that person has been and still is, without reinforcing that person's dependence. With the increasing population of those reaching later years, there will be an increasing need for guardians, most of them peers of those being "guarded." Volunteer guardians now are being trained for partial guardianship assistance by state associations, churches, and neighborhoods in conjunction with states' attorney generals and local legal associations. Up until the guarded person needs institutionalization, these volunteers serve a great purpose, for they furnish companionship and valuable assistance in facilitating semi-independence and options not otherwise open to the aging person requiring help.

In the Age of Gerontocracy there will be a need for thousands of guardians and a concurrent necessity to monitor state laws and update them through legislative action when needed. Some states do not require medical evidence of incompetency to be submitted to the court, and twenty-four states recognize senility or advanced age as basis for declaring incompetency. They leave it to the judge to decide. In many states the language defining guardianship responsibilities or even *guardian* leaves a helpless ward at the mercy of varying degrees of incompetent guarding. It is even possible in some situations for any person, even a criminal, to be appointed as guardian where the law is outdated or lacks clarity. The lack of supervision and of evaluation of a guardian often leaves a ward open to neglect. Mismanagement, embezzlement, or misappropriation can drain the ward's resources, leaving him or her totally dependent.

When persons are institutionalized, the civil rights of the wards become a critical issue within the larger issue. These persons are actually being transferred to a branch of government that will decide where they live, with whom they associate, what they will do each day, whether or not they will enter into contracts, and many other personal and civil privileges. Institutionalization even deprives them of control over money or property. Older persons without families are especially at risk.

As to the guardians, most states require only that they "act in the best interests of their wards," a virtually unenforceable standard. Institutional care is more open to the scrutiny of residents and family than is the private home, and laws generally offer some protection for institutional cases if the means of enforcing the laws are used. But within a home where the invasion of privacy prevents much reporting of abuse, the question becomes a troubling one, both legally and morally. This issue relates very closely to caregiving, and presents a major concern for policy makers in the Age of Gerontocracy. Seven guidelines accepted by the American Bar Association several years ago offer direction for concentrated efforts to remedy this complex problem.[10] Elders must be informed, for securing healthy guardianship is intimately connected to their peers and to their own lives. Questions such as these must be asked: What laws exist in each state or at the federal level relating to the custody of wards? Are public guardians qualified for their task? Are there limitations on the power of the guardians? What does the law *state* that they are to do? How are guardians supervised and evaluated?

Funding to provide adequate staff to respond to the reporting of any abuse and enough staff to offer the guidance and counseling needed to follow up on reports and results is a requisite. Finding some moral answer to this issue means a better, less fearful life for older persons requiring various degrees of assistance. At eighty-five, I am learning more about searching and seeking for the best sources for helping and remedying this problem.

Caregiving. In this chapter we will view caregiving with an emphasis upon its success in creating a morality of caring and of giving to helpless individuals, whatever their age. Perhaps the Age of Gerontocracy will find ways for discovering and designing more humane caretaking experiences for both the caretaker and the caregiver. Perhaps help can be found for individuals caught in the bind between personal life and life for another, as well as for a society that is presently the loser in a conflict between caregiving and pursuit of personal/career interests. Society now loses the contributions of those who have no time to pursue personal interests because they are caring for another, and the health of a stressed caregiver presents a risk of great hazards, both financial and psychological. Family structures, needed to form a secure base where loyalties and trust are established early in life, often cannot stand the strain of caregiving situations, and a question such as, "Whose house is this?" can tear the family apart to the point of divorce. This nation requires the strength of family relationships for its own perpetuity as a united people; the Age of Gerontocracy has a high stake in this whole issue of caregiving, and the results depend upon creative and imaginative endeavors and better answers than we have found so far. This is a national crisis, and immediate action is demanded. This has become, for me at eighty-five, a leading priority, along with its companion, guardianship.

Two million caregivers are giving care to one-and-one-half million seriously impaired individuals over the age of sixty-five. One-third of the caregivers (according to one study) were over sixty-five themselves; seventy-two percent were females, primarily wives, daughters, and daughters-in-law, and their own health was a matter of concern to them. Many older women will care for their spouses or loved ones during final illnesses, and then they face the next step— their own dying—alone. Often, they are without adequate financial resources. The family is being used as a cop out, for while home care is often desired by family and patient, such care is largely untrained, and the home is not effectively constructed to provide the care that is needed. No one intentionally becomes a caregiver; we back into the situation because it is thrust upon us, usually without warning or preparation. Great stress results, especially upon that member who must assume the major obligations, and the one providing the continuous caring, day in and day out, months on end, receives little if any financial or psychological relief. (Even federal legislation is a stopgap at best.)

In this chapter, caregiving is reemphasized because of the dare to succeed aspect that focuses upon the potential loss to society and to the individual in the failure to achieve personal goals and achievements. In giving up a career—or a job with earning power, or even in curtailing the hours of work, often without pay—the caregiver is placed in a precarious position concerning health and financial security. At this time of life, when caregivers had anticipated a time for new and innovative learning experiences or for beginning a second career, the stressful, if dutiful, caregiving for which they are largely unprepared becomes their lot in life. For many older women it will mean giving up advancement in a chosen career with a subsequent loss to her society and the personal loss of her own financial future. Social Security, which is a base for her financial resources, may suffer through unemployment since Social Security is an earned rights income and depends upon a stated period of work experience. More and more men are becoming caregivers as their spouses become victims of Alzheimer's disease or other disabling illnesses. Long-term care insurance is hard to obtain in the later years, and its cost is practically prohibitive, so men and women are now facing almost certain caregiving obligations. The answer would seem to be to work for and to work out a feasible program for long-term care as a governmentally administered program, with its expense shared as is Medicare, and to make it within the reach of all our citizens. Such a plan has been and is being discussed in Congress, and intensive pursuit of such a program for our nation's people is imperative.

The New Old. This is a phenomenon peculiar to this time of extended life; adult children in their sixties and seventies with parents in their eighties and nineties, even over one hundred, find themselves facing serious problems in the later years of both. Each is dependent upon the other, and neither is capable of assuming this responsibility. The caregiver, even with love and genuine caring, becomes a hostage to possible future poverty and ill health. Caregivers, and those cared for, need to be able to grasp every opportunity to live life to its fullest, for we do not have a second shot at it. This is the time for the elders, and it must count for them and for the society that *they* will make for themselves and others.

During these years when I have had the time to work at being old, I have noticed with growing concern, the waste of our "elderhood" as they become shut in, either at home or in a retirement community or a nursing home. I have a deepening sense of a lack of morality in making such persons become "shut outs," and I believe there is a wrongness about this that will undermine our future morality. The Age of Gerontocracy should turn its attention to the creative means whereby these thousands of "benched" players who have been a part—an important part—of the world we enjoy, are needed now to preserve the continuity of our own lives and experiences. Through electronic devices, through the telephone, and through dictated stories and testimonies, they can continue to make contributions to the world they helped to make. I recall talking to a resident in a health care center some years ago who was dying of cancer. Beside her pillow she had a tape recorder and she told me, with real joy, that she was telling that recorder a sequential account of her life from the moment when she knew of her condition—how she felt, how scared she was, what thoughts tore her apart, how others had helped her, how music had replaced many uncertainties, and how she had lost her fear of dying. Her telling of this to the tape made the situation real, made it a learning experience, and helped her to deal with it rationally. She was going to give the tape to her church library for any help it could give to others facing her problem or facing the event of dying. Her face showed no strain, and her voice was clear as she talked about something that many cannot and will not face. This woman, like others facing severe health problems, is still *in* the world, giving to it as she finds, in the giving, more of herself and what she *can* be.

The Sandwich Generation. This, too, is a phenomenon of this Age of Gerontocracy. With the exploding population of those over age fifty-five, many persons find themselves in their forties sandwiched in between older and younger generations, without lives of their own. They are parents both to their children and to their mothers and fathers who are temporarily or permanently impaired by age or disease. Realizing that they, too, will need care one day, but reluctant to put their children in their positions, these caregivers worry about their own futures as well. The Age of Gerontocracy needs to assess this situation morally, searching for ways to give a life back to those caught in the middle.

The Minority Elderly. In this chapter we dare to succeed as we view the minority elderly as enriching our heritage. In the minority society, the family is a strong social force, and although the family network is often not a sure base of support, having kin nearby holds no promise nor guarantee of available supportive help, either. In the minority population, projected to grow 283 percent by 2030, assistance other than the family or tribe will be needed to bolster the limited resources of family or kin.[11]

> Poverty for the ethnic minority elderly has its roots in historical factors such as discrimination, cultural and language differences, lower educational attainment, underemployment, employment in low-paying and irregular occupations such as factory or service work and farm labor, reductions in entitlement programs to the elderly population in general, and taxing policies which have favored the more affluent. Attention must be given to sources of social, cultural, and policy imbalances early on to remove their negative impact.[12]

With the help of these minority elders, we must explore and develop their untapped potential for enriching our entire social, religious, political, and cultural heritage. Above all, in the coming years when age rules by numerical influence, we must avoid age segregation that causes competing policies. We must address elderly needs in the context of the community as a whole—to benefit all, regardless of age or ethnic affiliation.

Abuse. We must look at the issue of abuse not only from the standpoint of facing the consequences if we allow it to continue; we must succeed in the hope that this destructive act can be outlawed under careful study and action. The issue of abuse (of the elderly, of youth, of children, and of spouses) is largely a hidden and ignored problem, especially within the home and family. The abused elderly are reluctant to admit that their children, loved ones, and those entrusted with their care have assaulted or neglected them. In reality, many cannot admit it because the privacy of the family and the home make it almost impossible to get the word out. The state laws usually mandate the reporting of abuse, but the inability to gather information, even to get someone to make an accusation, causes road blocks in the pursuance of investigations. The Age of Gerontocracy has an awesome responsibility to review laws that deal with abuse and to revise language and intent that agitate injustices.

Abuse is inherent in many dependent situations—the family, institutions, and caregiving. The victim is generally seventy-five years of age or older, female, and in some position of dependency. Victims accept abuse in silence because of shame, fear, reprisal by the abusers, or they fear being abandoned or institutionalized. Each year about one and a half million elderly, or one in twenty, are abused by their families or caregivers. Some of the abuse is unintentional, but, rather, the result of accumulated stress of a caregiver—or of the care receiver. Elder abuse falls into three general categories: acts of abuse, neglect, and exploitation. Incidents of abuse are recurring rather than remaining isolated single events and they generally occur over a period of five years or until the death of the abused puts an end to it. The Age of Gerontocracy needs to focus upon collecting data on the evidence of abuse of elder persons—or of any age—in every state so as to draw some valid and reliable conclusions that can lead to "putting teeth" into reporting laws and procedures.

The Elderly Homeless. One study[13] asks the question, How many homeless people are there in the U.S.? Disputed estimates range from 300,000 to 3 million. The Urban Institute was hired to make a study of the subject, and this study concludes that "we have in this country between 567,000 and 600,000 homeless people, most of them men, approximately half of them nonwhite." It would seem fair to assume that a proportionate part of this number—perhaps fifteen percent—is elderly. In many towns and cities now the street people are being housed overnight in churches and by agencies when winter comes, but a deeper ethical issue possessing moral and spiritual overtones is "Why does this situation exist in *this* nation?" The next fifty years may see an increase in the numbers of homeless elders, and, in fact, of entire families. A new spirit of hope and faith in this nation and its people would arise if we could find some solutions to this situation, and presently displaced persons could relate positively and resourcefully to a society that compassionately welcomes this issue as a charge to keep—with dignity and honor.

The Older Woman. A force to be reckoned with, the older woman presents a challenge to capitalize upon her great potential as a contributing power in the Age of Gerontocracy. Her numbers and her varied abilities, as well as her knowledge, skills, and values as both homemaker and career woman combine to furnish the coming century with a diverse source of immeasurable and invaluable strength. She will have an unpredictable impact upon this time in history, depending upon her readiness for and incentive to interject a new vitality and a new perception into her society. The Older Women's League points out the seven social concerns that in the near future may have to be reconsidered with the changing feminization of our society: health care, pension rights, jobs for older women, Social Security reforms, support for family services, federal budget priorities, and staying in control to the end of life.

Who is the older woman? What is she like? How does she feel about herself? She may be widowed, living alone, divorced, living in an institution, or living on the street. She may be a receiver of assistance or a producer and donor of her invaluable experience as an independent, creative, resourceful, and achieving person, interested and interesting. The potential is great, both for her own self-realization and for her world.

Of the estimated number of Americans who are now at least one hundred years old, approximately three-fourths are women. Women in the over sixty-five age bracket are growing rapidly in number. The Older Women's League several years ago showed that older women outnumber older men by 7 million, outregister men by 4.7 million, and outvote men by 4 million. These ratios will rise as the population of elders rises. Many older women are heads of households without the benefits that normally go with this position. The older woman has substantially lower income and is more dependent upon entitlements and social services programs than are men. Poverty is the older woman's problem, and cuts in those programs upon which she depends have undermined her previous security. Recent uncertainties in regard to Social Security and Medicare/Medicaid related to the budget deficit, have produced anxieties that are traumatic and threaten the very basis of her existence. To dare to succeed is to free her from her fears and to open up new avenues for exploration and achievement of her potential for empowered productivity and accomplishment.

For many women the poverty is faced alone, without family members to provide social, emotional, or financial support; and in these days of greater longevity, there is resultant concern for preparing for her own aging, as well as caring for a spouse or older frail relative whose care requires that she stay at home, losing her opportunity to work and earn money to supplement her income. Her various roles in life may not qualify her for her own pension; also, the death of her

111

spouse may leave her without health protection at a time when she cannot afford the premiums. The "widow's gap" in Social Security catches many widows unaware; her age may serve as a discriminatory factor in having a job terminated or in not getting one at all; the older woman's needs are special and must be so considered.

The coming generations of older women will not be alike; the times in which each generation lives and the years from which they have drawn their experiences create provocative and distinctive differences in what they offer. But when the Baby Boomers peak in 2030, "oldness" will have certain attributes that are common to all elders, men and women, and the elders will share a common vulnerability. How much has society made constructive use of their knowledge and wisdom, with each being a precious life packet of individualized learning, and how have these been incorporated into society's structure? Has their oldness discarded them—rejected them because the stereotype, perpetuated by them and their world, has forced them into inactivity, disuse, and retirement? Older women are not more important than older men, but there are more of them, and this numerical influence makes them the major determiner of the entire quality of life in the Age of Gerontocracy. To dare to succeed will create a new force for productive accomplishment that has been lacking in our world in previous times, and we must latch on to this resource *now*.

Education. Finally, but embracing all other issues is education, which will necessarily occupy a central position in the coming years. Attitudes will have to change among those elders who still consider that "these days, if it ain't fun, we don't do it." Furthermore, having lived in and been educated in a past, the policy makers for the future will need new learnings for new issues and problems. Erroneous decisions could result from incorrect or incomplete information. Elders will have to make momentous decisions about situations relating to the present and the future, while the basis for judgment is not relevant to current problems. Personal bias, inherited from the past, may put blinders on them, or apathy may turn them away from anything that challenges motivation to change.

Education will have to be academic and social in nature. It is projected now that a dynamic economy, offering jobs to workers entering the labor market, depends upon quality education.

Education lays the foundation for a work force with the skills demanded by new technologies and developing businesses. States have recognized the link between education and the economy . . . and (have) responded with "initiatives geared toward innovation and excellence in such areas as early childhood education, dropout prevention, adult literacy, and vocational training."[14]

It should be added that because of the force of the older citizens in the Age of Gerontocracy, education for leadership *by them* is a requisite.

Aging is normal and natural and has to be accepted as inevitable and a reality, a creative experience for those who make a career out of aging, unrewarding and destructive for those who deny aging as part of life. Birth, growth, decline, cessation appear throughout all of nature, and human beings are no exception. Education must prepare a person for this life process, with the parallel sense of fulfillment, self-achievement, and self-value at each stage of life. "Becoming what is possible for me" is difficult, if not impossible, in a society where invidious comparisons with models beyond my attainment make me a failure as myself. It would be difficult for me, for example, to reach eighty-five believing that God loves me, if all along the way God's world has rejected me.

For teenagers and young adults education has to teach them the skills with which to manage life—life at their age, not at some future time; for they live now, and today provides the only arena for their learning what to do with their world. Accomplishment and achievement or failure are their report card for further efforts, especially for their motivations and their goals. Pre-retirement education and planning need to prepare the young adult to preview the future possibilities and probabilities, to sample and explore ways in which to deal realistically with change and its attendant crises—to rehearse retirement in practical situations, and to prepare alternative choices for individual problem situations.

For us, the elders, education must be continuing and continuous, enabling us to survive with genuine meaning, purpose, and dignity; to cope intelligently and courageously with inevitable change, even to welcome it as a test of our ability to manage it constructively; to give generously and gratefully of our special abilities; to grow up into a confident sense of being; and to know that we are in one piece as someone who likes being "me." Our two principal fears—solitude and loss of independence—need not be grim faces of strangers to us, for, in growing up, we have seen them for what they are, and they are familiar company who, along the way, have afforded us with an education in how to meet them and live with them. Therefore, they do not frighten us, but, rather, offer us possibilities for exploration of untried experiences and for moving forth into uncertainties of the unknown on our own or with others.

The education of the older American must, for self-protection, provide political knowledge and know-how since our very existence is based in the political system wherein we function. For example, a form of government may guarantee freedom of worship, and its citizens may worship or refrain from worship as they wish. But if the form of government is changed for us by others, the new government may well deny the freedom of worship, may impose a form of worship upon us, or forbid religious expression on pain of persecution and death for disobedience. A people must be educated for the exercise of their freedom and keep themselves informed, being watch dogs and monitoring events and policies to safeguard their rights.

In this time of the age-oriented ballot box, the votes of the older citizens are power votes. Age fifty-five and its increasing numerical majority become the growing force that has in its discretion the determination of what happens politically in the present and casts long shadows ahead into the years when, through the "geriatric echo," their policies and decisions will still affect greatly the lives of generations yet unborn. In exercising the right and the privilege to vote, the older citizens are using a franchise denied to multitudes around the world, and which they, too, deny through apathy and indifference when they do not *choose* to vote. Any vote, important as it is, should be exercised with care, with thoughtful preparation, and with an earnest search for accurate and credible information, based in authentic, respected, and unbiased sources. The media become extremely important in how they present a candidate and that candidate's platform and political record. To make a sound and wise choice, the voter must sift fact from fiction, truth from misrepresentation. A voter will need to be educated as to tactics used to mislead and distort facts, so as to make decisions in which trust is not betrayed.

As major consumers for the next century, the expanding older market makes the elders especially susceptible to crime, to fraud, to abuse. Older persons, in self-protection, will need to examine intelligently and systematically decisions of importance to them and their communities. They must find out how to prevent exploitation by those who would use them to further their personal goals.

Education for religious, spiritual, moral, and ethical maturity to match the age of the citizens and the age in which they are the policy makers must furnish the support for their decisions and for the power that the elders will exert. The church will depend upon its older members as never before, because youth will not be around in numbers strong enough to create the leadership that society will be needing in critical times ahead. The Age of Gerontocracy is largely an uncharted experience, and institutional religion will need its elders to provide that moral and spiritual leadership if a matured faith is to become a dynamic factor in our world. Education for responsive and responsible leadership in the next century will demand information that is accurate and reliable from proven sources, a high degree of motivation, and a matured faith that has grown as the person has grown, a "faith that does not shrink" in good times or in bad.

Aging persons must also educate themselves to face the reality of death. Throughout this section on education, the focus has been upon education for life and living, but inevitably life here does cease, and everyone faces or denies this in very personal ways. It is strange to hear someone say, "If I die, be sure to . . ." with a request for something to be done in a certain way. There is no "if" about the condition of death—it is not a matter of choice. To say, "when I die" makes death real, recognizable, and something to consider thoughtfully and with planning wherever possible. Many people ignore or skirt this issue as if by refusing to think of or talk about it, it will go away. Our very language retreats from facing it: "she passed on," or "he left us today" evade the real fact that somebody died, is dead, and this is a fact of life. "The recognition of our own mortality may be said to be the characteristic that separates human beings from all other creatures on this earth."[15] The concept of death affects life itself. Try to imagine a life without death. Is there a "rational mortality"? "A deathless universe would be a lifeless one, for life as we know it, gets its vitality, its intensity from its own temporary perishability."[16] Death, as a reality throughout the world, makes it seem to be an ordinary, day-by-day event to which we become hardened unless it happens to us. Every day, death comes into our homes from a television program or a radio commentary, with the daily newspaper—a battlefield, a terrorist bombing, a plane crash, a tornado, or a fire. Heretofore, we have had to live with individual death—one person killing another person. From now on, we will be reckoning with the fact that death as a species is an eventuality to be expected, a nation eradicating another, whole peoples ceasing to exist.[17]

The democracy of death makes all of us sharers in a common event, but each has his or her own time, place, and means of dying, and each person has his or her own style.

The terminal stage of life merits and offers opportunities for the experience and expression of some of the most significant aspects of humanness: courage, audacity, determination, faith, humor, compassion, unselfishness, sensitivity to others—all are possible when we draw near to our own mortality. It is then that one is afforded the final chance to create personal meaning, for the communication of the integrity of one's life to those left behind. It provides the final, unique opportunity to express one's ultimate belief in the future as a continuum of growth wherever and whatever that future may be.[18]

Death brings us face to face with an inescapable reality, for whether we learn to live longer—one hundred years or more—death does put a period to it at some time. Whatever added years are allotted, these years afford a person the time to live richly, expectantly, and fully, bringing to the death event the challenge of meaning.

Elisabeth Kübler-Ross effectively encompasses aspects of death and dying.[19] Our natural reactions may be to deny death, to bargain with the Almighty, to retreat from reality into substitute activity, to accept with a degree of serenity that which is inevitable. With the Supreme Court's ruling (June 1990) relating to euthanasia, many elders now desire to choose their time and place for dying, especially when their own death or that of a loved one is to be agonizing or degrading, or if the cost of staying alive and healthy is prohibitive, making them hostages to poverty.

So education for death is a recognized need today and in the Age of Gerontocracy. But this should not and must not make unimportant or irrelevant the living of life to its fullest—to finding a potential self that has not yet come into being. Whatever one's attitude is toward life and/or death, making a career out of aging causes us to confront squarely the fact of death; for death is there, either with an immature philosophy of life or with a tested faith and confidence.

I have called death life's most creative event, perhaps a startling idea for some, shocking for others. Consider that it occurs only once to any person, and, thus, it is new, never before experienced by the person, and never to be repeated. It is original to each individual; each one makes a personal statement, rare and genuine.

But chiefly, death is the culminating event of what we call life, and, as that culmination, it becomes the reflection of a continuing and continuous self, either of one who, in life, achieved no sense of worth and identity, or as one who, throughout life, discovered who he or she is, where each is going, and why he or she has been here. In this normal and expected climax is the opportunity for the creation of personal meaning, a testament to a becoming and a being *all* that is possible. Now is the time for the integrity of life itself to be communicated to those left behind who have been and are part of the life and death events. Depending upon one's spiritual and religious beliefs, death is the final chance to express one's ultimate conviction that life has been a gift for a time, an apprenticeship, that it has purpose and plan, and that it has made a difference because it has been a promise kept, or betrayed, as the case may be. Thus, death becomes an affirmation and the diploma for admission into the next adventure of learning and achievement, a new unique creation formed *by* and *in* death from what life has brought to this creative act of dying. Perhaps we are not in control of the when nor the how of our dying, but we do largely control the what—the results and all that we have been, are, and can be to become the legacy to those who outlive us.

The Church. Since the Age of Gerontocracy creates a new power dimension throughout the entire societal structure, affecting every aspect of it from industry and the national economy to the local community with its moral obligations to its members, a major question faces this age: What does institutional religion have to do with this emerging demographic shift in population, and how is this effect felt? (The "church" is used in the following pages to refer to the "church universal," the ecumenical church, in whatever way humanity relates to a Deity, whether in a Protestant setting, in a temple, a cathedral, a synagogue, under a desert sky on windswept sands, in a meeting house, as a "community of faith," or a "fellowship.") This church is the major force in the society for spiritual, ethical, and moral guidance and instruction that, until now, no other institution has assumed. As that directing force, it will be a different church from a youth-oriented one; its human and material resources will necessarily be those of its aging majority—those in the later years of life, requiring education for a new role of leadership, of initiator and of activator. The 1990's as the "Trend Era" will give us a breathing space—ten years of vision to create a century of change, and we must immediately discover and develop the power potential of the experienced, underused Larger Generation to begin to carry out their new role to match the new age.

No longer can such a Larger Generation with its seventy to ninety million (before the years 2030 to 2040) be considered as an entity. Within this entity are millions of individual lives that make living history, and they must not be wasted. Education will need to focus on individual possibilities to find ways to involve the elders in self-discovery, self-achievement, self-realization. Each generation sequentially contributes to those before and after, and each has a limitless reservoir of individuals full of highly personalized capabilities and attainments. This 1990 era of preparation will find the shifting demographics both a liability and an asset: by 2025, Americans over sixty-five will outnumber teenagers by two to one, and by the middle of the century, one out of four persons will be over sixty-five. Those aged fifty-five to sixty-four, now numbering 22 million, will show a ten percent increase in ten years; ages sixty-five to seventy-four, now 17 million, will have a ten percent increase in ten years; the seventy-five to eighty-four age bracket now number 11 million, and there will be a twenty-five percent increase in ten years. Note this! The eighty-five and older, now numbering 2.7 million, will, within the next ten years, show a fifty percent increase! These are the "old old." About seventy percent of this group is made up of older women, with more than sixty percent widowed, and twenty-four percent living in some health care facility or other institution.[20]

In 1980 there were only 15,000 centenarians in the entire country. In 1990 there were 54,000, and by the year 2000, there will be 100,000 Americans at least one hundred years old. There are so many centenarians that they have their own organization called the American Centenarian Committee.

This unprecedented population explosion will present the ecumenical church with its greatest challenge and its greatest risk, depending upon whether the ministry provided for the education of older members is a magnet drawing from them their individual life experiences, or whether it is a reinforcement of their "dependency" inadequacies. If the latter happens, then the church and other religious forces will be relegated to the sidelines, lacking the significance to make any real difference in a world needing a dynamic spiritual direction.

In 1900, a life expectancy was 47.3 years; in 1984-85, it was 74.7, and it is extending as we learn how to live longer. The troubling question for me is, expectancy for what? For in extending the life expectancy of our people, do we also give them a better life?—one of security and personal worth? What does it benefit a person to live longer if that life is filled with rejection, a sense of unworthiness, of failure? The question, "expectancy for what?" leads into an uncomfortable search for an answer that can be morally, ethically, and spiritually satisfying. Here is where the church faces the dare to fail and its consequences.

In this age-oriented religious heritage, the intergenerational legacy will be dependent upon the continuity of youth and age as joint creators and administrators of that heritage. But it will be the elders who will have to generate the ideas, be the doers and makers, initiate actions, and produce the services for many of their own peers, serving as well as being served. In the age of emphasis upon a growing rebirth of morality, there will be loaded issues that will dare the older generations to fail and to succeed. Much information will be demanded, and elders will have to adopt a motivating urgency to get ready for their new role. A growing faith that has matured with their chronological age has to give the older policy makers a sense of support and sustenance to guide them in the uncertain future that is theirs.

Inheritance and Legacy. Inheritance and legacy are two sides of the same coin, for what a generation has inherited becomes that generation's special legacy as it creates a future from its own past and present experiences. The date of January 16, 1991, the day the war in the Persian Gulf began, thus becomes a time to remember as possessing an inherent poignancy, a nostalgic lingering look at a time gone forever, and a future holding many unknowns that the elders face as the decision makers in time of war and its aftermath of peace. Elders, accustomed to envisioning retirement years as their time to do as they wish, to choose their way of life, now find this time to be one of serious involvement in a world unlike any planned or imagined by them.

This is not to say that the elders are unacquainted with war and its consequences, for many of them fought in and lived through two World Wars, the undeclared Korean conflict, the Vietnam War (a conscience-troubling experience for them and their society), and years of a "cold war" threat and persistent anxiety. Domestic crises of racial bitterness, educational inequalities, poverty, drugs, crime in the streets, unemployment, and financial insecurity have been their teachers in the school of experience.

These disturbing events occurred when the elders were young enough to expect such challenges, but at this later time of life they find their position of numerical power presenting them with demands for which they feel unprepared. As the participating majority in a society now expecting from them a new role in a new age of elderhood, they must find whatever answers and solutions there are. The store of knowledge is expanding far beyond much of the dated education that a generation possesses; even the vocabulary is bewildering, almost a foreign language. Apathy and disinterest may lessen the motivation, and many of the problems seem unsolvable.

The reality that war had come again in 1991 was, for some, difficult to accept. It requires from older persons continuing learning, a deep commitment to their new role, and a faith "to move mountains." The problems are their inheritance—they go with the territory of living where and when they do; and the church, as the moral and spiritual leader for society, will need to determine what its involvement is, as the moral and spiritual leader desperately needed in the coming centuries.

Knowledge, wisdom, and motivation to act will be required as elderhood tries to find answers where no answers seem possible. Consider the rising crisis of liberated peoples who are unused to the disciplines and education that liberation requires; homelessness of displaced persons everywhere; the children without a childhood; a deteriorated moral, ethical, and spiritual perceptiveness in both personal and government conduct; national and international drug abuse and crime that are a threat to the total global security; terrorism and its use of human blackmail and degradation; a technology that possesses the potential for both destroying our earth and for healing the manifold ills of that earth; and domestic crises of racial discrimination, of minority injustices, of the attendant waste of irreplaceable human possibilities.

There, in our inheritance, is the war-diminished manpower, and the emerging realization that we may find the answer in the strength and leadership of women, even possibly a women's military. We must look at the need for family stability as the fundamental training ground for our national strength and security; and we must look at economic progress and discover how to make compatible the woman's place in the work force with her increasing role as a caregiver. We must address the reinforcement of dependency of the following in the elderly majority whose leadership is critical to our society's management and progress: agricultural regenerative processes to ensure the productivity, safety, and beauty of our ravaged environment; alternative sources of energy that are safe, available, and affordable; and Space, and our treatment of it. We must consider the January 1991 war, the victory after this conflict, and the attendant crises relating to refugees with nowhere to go: the resettlements and boundaries; the reparations and some guarantees against the horrors of nuclear weaponry; the child victims of war and of peace, and their lost youth; devastated forest lands, polluted water, unbreathable air; the wounded and maimed victims; and the prisoners of war—these are only a few of the realities of elderhood's inheritance and the legacy we hand on to the future. Education for life and for death will lead us to "green pastures" where individual differences, instead of creating barriers between people, will intensify and enhance in those very differences our common and collective strengths. With a "faith to move mountains," the Age of Gerontocracy may bring into being as its legacy a time when "they shall beat their swords into plowshares, and their spears into pruning hooks;" where "nation shall not lift up a sword again nation, neither shall they learn war any more" (Micah 4:3, RSV). What a legacy!

Time is an asset and a liability. For there is time to spend, time to waste, and time to invest; time, unlike money, cannot be put away to be saved for a rainy day, and in these later years, time goes by and becomes precious. Newly-retired persons may feel lost with their newly found free time—an estimated 2000 hours per year that were previously work-oriented. In the pre-retirement years, a person usually looks forward to the free time, but when one feels no longer needed, time can hang heavy on one's hands. Time can be an enemy, creating emptiness and feelings of withdrawal, apathy, self-induced illness, depression, drug dependency, alcoholism, even suicide. However, free time used creatively can provide unlimited chances for developing new interests, for brushing up on old skills, for self-enrichment, for personal achievement, and for experiencing things heretofore only dreamed of. Time *invested* leads the individual into new paths of interesting involvement, of expanded learning, of new relationships, and of developing of inner strength. The church certainly must realize that a "luncheon-trip" type of ministry for the "investing" elders is not sufficient unto the challenge; the church must see an individual, and must see the aging generations as the potential dynamics of the coming century for the church and its society. Church and society must rethink any former positions that have become a pattern of behavior that are no longer helpful or progressive. We will need to recapture our vision of what can be and must be.

A suggested plan of action for reinvestment of time for those readers who view the Age of Gerontocracy as their time of reinvestment:

1. Be aware. An issue rises out of concerns, often personal and local. Examples: drugs, crime, abuse, education.

2. Seek out and join others with similar reactions and form alliances; or join groups already in action.

3. Get legislators involved and help to educate in the legislative process so that the action taken is an informed action. Get the legislature interested and involved in the problem and its solution.

4. Arouse public interest through the media.

5. Set public meetings wherein opponents and proponents present all aspects of the issue; write letters, speak out, monitor what is happening in the legislature relating to the issue. Check on the legislative history of any previous bill related to the issue—what was the result of such previous action?

6. Get the legislation introduced. The public must understand how this is done so that the people may participate at the proper time.

7. The legislation is passed or rejected (or amended).

8. It becomes law or fails. If passed, a "new morality" is introduced into society through acceptance, for the law stamps the new proposals with its legal approval, and it is now "right" and "good" under the law.

Learning to be all the ages that have been my stairsteps to reaching this time of life has caused me to make a career out of aging. Those who have viewed their years in this way—as a career—have, without being conscious of it, perhaps seen change as subversive in many ways: it disturbs the status quo, it shakes familiar foundations, it "rocks the boat," and it makes us uneasy. But change forces us to rethink our former positions and recapture our vision of what can be and should be. The Age of Gerontocracy, a once-in-history occurrence with its geriatric echo creating a long shadow into the future, can turn the world around. It does not seem plausible to think that this "gray power" has happened by accident—that for this one time in history such a potential for achievement and enrichment of the society is here by chance. Rather, it seems that we, as that Larger Generation, that longevity revolution,21 are here at this particular time and place in history marked as a people of destiny, a people called to a purpose and a mission all our own. Certainly, it is at such a time as this that the story of a young queen in biblical history carries real meaning.

You remember the story: Confronted in her youth with an awesome responsibility, the young Queen Esther was ordered by her Uncle Mordecai to go to the king, her husband, to plead for the life of her people. Esther understandably hesitated and reminded her uncle that if she went in unbidden to the king, and if he did not hold out his scepter to her, she would forfeit her life. Then it was that Mordecai spoke the word that holds special significance to the Age of Gerontocracy. He asked Esther a question that confronts the older generations today in their time of power and influence: "Who knows whether you have not come to the kingdom for such a time as this?" (Esther 4:14, RSV).

How do we know that we are not here just for this time? This we do know—we have stepped into history as have millions of others of our elders, and we will be here in growing numbers as an expanding force to effect change of some sort. If we dare to fail, to re-engage ourselves in the dynamic process of living and accomplishing—if we "retire," then we leave a retired world as our legacy, and we leave the world as its debtor.

When we search through the Bible for levels of motivation, Genesis 5:27 tells us that Methuselah lived nine hundred sixty and nine years, and then he died—a level of pure existence, just being here and passing the time. But the Age of Gerontocracy demands more. A higher level is found in Galatians 4:28 (RSV) in Paul's letter to the fellowship at Galatia: "We . . . like Isaac, are children of promise." But promises are not enough for the next century—promises are pledges but not accomplishments. They have to be kept for something to happen. And when our humanness begins to show as we point out that we can't be expected to continue in the ways of our youth because our energy simply isn't up to it, we are prodded by Isaiah 40:31 (RSV): "They who wait for the Lord shall renew their strength, they shall mount up with wings like eagles, they shall run and not be weary, they shall walk and not faint." We know we are not in this alone. And we take Luke 3:15 (NEB) as our theme for action, as the stage is set for the next century and for its Age of Gerontocracy: We are a generation standing "on the tiptoe of expectation."

Listen again to the question asked of Esther: "And who knoweth whether *thou* art come to the kingdom for such a time as this" (Esther 4:14, KJV, italics mine).

May these words from the hymn "God of Grace and God of Glory" guide us forward in the living of our mission: "Grant us wisdom, grant us courage, for the living of these days."

Notes

1. Welch, Elizabeth. *Sunday's Child,* Row, Peterson, and Company, Evanston, Il. 1944.

2. Oldham, Etta Baldwin. "Jis' Blue," in *Poetry Arranged for the Speaking Choir,* Marion Parsons Robinson and Rozetta Lura Thurston. Expression Co., Boston, 1936, p. 339.

3. Commager, Henry Steele. *The American Mind: An Interpretation of American Thought and Character Since the 1880's.* New Haven: Yale University Press, 1950, pp. 442-443.

4. Thayer, Lloyd. "Social Security File," *PARADE* Magazine, March 18, 1990.

5. Melcher, John. "A Separate CPI for Elders." *Generations,* Public Policy, Spring 1988, p. 74.

6. Shearer Lloyd. *Intelligence Report, PARADE* Magazine, November 29, 1987, p. 13;
   Lockery, Shirley A. "Care in the Minority Family," *Generations,* Fall 1985, p. 27.

7. Jessup, Denise and Greenberg, Barbara. "Innovative Older Worker Programs," American Society on Aging, *Generations,* Business and Aging, Summer 1989, pp. 23-27.

8. "Mother's Day Report 1989," *The OWL Observer,* Older Women's League, June/July 1989, p. 1.

9. Woestindick, Jo. "When They Are Forty," *Winston-Salem Journal,* Winston-Salem, N.C., July 22, 1990, G3.

10. American Bar Association, Commission on Legal Problems of the Elderly. Approved by the ABA House of Delegates, August 1987.

11. Lockery, Shirley A., "Care in the Minority Family," *Generations,* Fall 1985, p. 27.

12. Lockery, Shirley A., "Minority Aged Income Policy," *Generations,* Public Policy, Spring 1988, p. 65.

13. Shearer, Lloyd. "The Homeless," *Intelligence Report, Parade Magazine,* December 18, 1988, p. 13.

14. Editorial, "Business and Education," *Winston-Salem Journal,* July 15, 1988, p. 8.

15. Stevens-Long, Judith. *Adult Life, Developmental Processes,* Mayfield Publishing Company, Colorado State University, 1979, p. 439.

16. Ibid., p. 441.

17. Ibid., p. 441.

18. Ibid., p. 472.

19. Kübler-Ross, Elisabeth. *On Death and Dying,* New York: Macmillan, 1969, Chapters 3-7.

20. General Board of Discipleship, TRENDS, No. 5, Vol. 5, Oct. 1987. United Methodist Church. Other denominations will have similar data for their age groups which provide a workable basis for planning.

21. Bronte, D. Lydia. "Transformation to an Aging Society," *Generations:* Public Policy Issue, Spring 1988, p. 32.

About the Author

Dr. Elizabeth Welch, of Winston-Salem, North Carolina, is the retired Chairperson of the Department of Psychology and Education at Salem College in Winston-Salem. She is Adjunct Professor of Psychology and Gerontology at Bowman Gray School of Medicine in Winston-Salem, and has taught in several North Carolina public school systems.

Dr. Welch is a popular keynote speaker at many national conferences on aging sponsored by The United Methodist Church and organizations such as the Shepherd's Centers of America. She has been a delegate to the White House Conference on Aging, and is politically active as an advocate on aging issues at the state and national levels.

She is a drama enthusiast and has won numerous awards for playwriting and production of dramas. She is an accompanist for the "Sharps and Flats," a musical group of twenty-four older persons who identify themselves as "Ambassadors of Creative Aging."

She is an active member of Centenary United Methodist Church in Winston-Salem.